INVITATION TO RANELAGH

JAMES BARTLEMAN ESQ:
Gentleman of His Majesty's Chapels Royal,
Died April 15.1821...Aged 52.

O--Lord have mercy O Lord up-on me

Sig: Pergolesi.

Engraved by W.H. Worthington

MOLLIE SANDS

INVITATION
TO RANELAGH
1742-1803

Hither Nymphs and Swains repair,
Quit the baleful scenes of strife,
Leave the rugged paths of care
And taste of joys that sweeten life.

INVITATION TO RANELAGH
SONG BY
MICHAEL ARNE 1780

JOHN WESTHOUSE
LONDON
1946

First published in December 1946 *by*

JOHN WESTHOUSE (PUBLISHERS) LTD
49 CHANCERY LANE LONDON W1

Printed in Great Britain by

GALE & POLDEN LTD
IDEAL HOUSE LONDON W.C.2

CONTENTS

ACKNOWLEDGMENTS

Grateful thanks are due to Mr. F. Geoffrey Rendall of the British Museum, for his friendly encouragement and expert help; to the Staff of the London Library, without whom the book could not have been written; to my Mother, and to Mrs. Hubert Edwards for her constructive criticism and kindly advice. The quotations from Leopold Mozart's letters are taken by kind permission of the publishers, Messrs. Macmillan and Co. Ltd., from the "Letters of Mozart and his Family, chronologically arranged and translated by Emily Anderson." The quotations from Horace Walpole's letters are from the Paget Toynbee edition, and are given by kind permission of The Clarendon Press, Oxford. Thanks are also due to the publishers of THE MONTHLY MUSICAL RECORD *for permission to reproduce certain material which has appeared in its columns.*

TO
BSJ
BMJS

FOREWORD

THE late Frank Kidson called the eighteenth-century London Pleasure Gardens ' the Nurseries of English Song,' and it is true that their rise in the 30's and 40's of the century did much to keep alive English song-writing and English singing when both were threatened with extinction by the Italian operatic style. Marylebone, Vauxhall, Cuper's and Ranelagh were pre-eminent for size and musical interest among the many Gardens which flourished in the outskirts of London in the last three-quarters of the century, and of these four perhaps Ranelagh makes the greatest appeal to the modern imagination. There is music in the very name – pronounced Runnelow in its heyday, while London itself was Lunnon. (Charles James Fox spoke of Lunnon to the last.)

This book at first set out to trace the careers of the chief singers associated with Ranelagh Gardens during its reign of sixty-odd years, from the early Handelian and operatic singers – John Beard, Tenducci, Charlotte Brent, Mrs. Arne – to Charles Dibdin, Incledon and Mme Mara at the end of the century. To write of the singers without saying something of the songs they sang, the composers who wrote those songs and the instrumentalists who accompanied them, proved impossible. Michael Festing, Dr. Arne, Dr. Boyce, James Hook,

Giardini, Barthelemon, the Ashley's, and many other musicians have their place in these pages. Nor can mention be omitted of a certain concert given in the summer of 1764 in aid of ' a Public useful charity,' at which ' a Child of 7 years of Age,' performed ' several fine select Pieces of his own Composition on the Harpsichord and on the Organ, which has already given the highest Pleasure, Delight and Surprize to the greatest Judges of Music in England or Italy,' the child in question being Wolfgang Amadeus Mozart. Ranelagh programmes were usually up to date ; in the first years Handel has pride of place, and he never entirely drops out, but the names of Dr. Arne, Dr. Boyce, James Hook, J. C. Bach, Avison, Corelli, Giardini, Abel, Charles Dibdin, and, finally, Haydn are added as the years go by. Audiences in the eighteenth century were not afraid of contemporary music.

Ranelagh is indeed no bad vantage point from which to survey the English musical world of 1742-1803. But the musical world does not exist independently. Music is not created in a vacuum, and musicians have to live, though this is often forgotten. The kind of music they write and perform is dependent upon the social, economic and even political conditions of their time. This was particularly so in the eighteenth century at a place of fashionable entertainment where the songs naturally reflected the manners, tastes and even the events of the day. Topical songs are not necessarily ephemeral. Few eighteenth century songs are so well-known to-day as Boyce's ' Heart of Oak,' yet it was a *pièce d'occasion* ; probably not many of those who sing lustily in chorus about ' the wonderful year ' have any notion what year is alluded to, or what happened to make it specially wonderful, and they cheerfully persist in singing of Hearts of Oak, but their appreciation of the song is none the less sincere.

The face of England and of Europe was to change greatly from that day in April, 1742, when the Rotunda and Gardens were first opened to the public until the buildings were pulled down in 1805. The year Ranelagh opened was the year in which Sir Robert Walpole fell. It was the end of that period of twenty years' apparent peace and prosperity, during which he had used every diplomatic wile to keep this country out of wars on the Continent, while he consolidated at home the Hanoverian dynasty and developed the Cabinet system of government. The new age into which Ranelagh was born was to be an age of imperial expansion and European commitments – the age of the elder Pitt, of Wolfe and Clive, and also of Frederick the Great, Maria Theresa and Louis XV. That age in turn passed into the Industrial Revolution, itself but the prologue to the revolutionary epoch, the rise of a new spirit in Europe, and a new threat to this island – the age of the younger Pitt, of Burke, of Fox, of Nelson, and also of Washington and Napoleon, of American Independence and the French Revolution. Ranelagh's first songs were sung when the German-born George II was on the throne, the War of the Austrian Succession was in progress and the Stuarts were preparing to make their last bid for the throne of their ancestors. Its last songs were sung during the reign of Farmer George, not long after the Peace of Amiens had called a brief halt to the Napoleonic struggle. Pope was still the most admired poet when Ranelagh opened, and *Lyrical Ballads* had been published before it closed.

Finally, the Ranelagh audiences must not be forgotten. Everyone who mattered in the English world from 1742 to 1803 strolled at some time through the Gardens by the Thames, or joined the throng that walked round and round the Rotunda – Dr. Johnson, Boswell, Laurence Sterne, Oliver Goldsmith, Sir Joshua Reynolds, Thomas Gray, Horace Walpole, Fielding, Richardson, members of the Royal family and governing classes, the Grenville's, the Russell's, the Cavendishes, the Duke of Newcastle, Henry Pelham, Lord Mansfield, Charles James Fox.

Canalet. delin.   Publish'd Accor...

*A View of the Canal, Chinese Building, Rotundo, &c.
in* RANELAGH GARDENS, *with the* MASQUERADE.

Printed for W...

THE CANAL, CHINESE HOUSE AND

rliament. 1769.   C. Grignion Sculp.

Vüe du Canal, du Bâtiment, Chinois, de la Rotunda, &c.
des JARDINS de RANELAGH un jour de MASQUARADE.

Sold by Mayor at the Golden Buck opposite Fetter Lane Fleet Street

ROTUNDA DURING A MASQUARADE

A serious study of the music, politics or social life of the eighteenth century is outside the scope of this work, and would be a poor tribute to the memory of a place of ' polite Amusement ' as the eighteenth century called it. But it is hoped that readers for whom this kind of essentially English *fête galante* has an attraction will not grudge a few hours spent in the company of ghosts so elegant and amiable, nor feel they have wasted time in accepting this Invitation to Ranelagh.

PROLOGUE

' WE hear the House and Gardens of the late Lord Ranelagh at Chelsea are purchased in order to make it a Place of Entertainment like Vauxhall against next Summer,' wrote a gossiping and doubtless ' inspired ' journalist in February, 1740, but it was to be two more years before Vauxhall's most formidable rival opened its doors. The fashionable village of Chelsea was a good choice as the site of a new Pleasure Garden, because it was renowned for the healthiness of its air. To mention only four of its many famous convalescents, the Earl of Essex moved there when he was ' sick ' in 1599 ; Swift wrote to Stella in 1711 that he planned ' to lodge at Chelsea for the air ' ; in 1749 Smollett brought his consumptive only child to Monmouth House ; and in 1764 Leopold Mozart nursed the remains of his ' cold ' in Fivefields Row. It had always been famous for its gardens. There was the Physic Garden, the garden of the Royal Hospital itself, and many another private garden, as well as the renowned nurseries along the ' King's Private Road.'

Chelsea Hospital had been completed in 1691, and before that date Lord Ranelagh had obtained several grants of land belonging to the institution which he developed into an ' elegantly designed garden,' opening into Chelsea College walks, and upon which he built a house of brick, cornered with stone. It was ' very fine within, all the rooms being wainscotted with Norway oak, and all the chimneys adorned with carvings, as in the Council Chamber of Chelsea College.'[1] Such was Ranelagh in December, 1691. When Lord Ranelagh died in 1712, the property passed to his unmarried daughter, and in 1730 it was vested in the hands of trustees. In 1733 it was sold in ten lots, and the house and grounds were purchased for £3,200 by Lacy (patentee of Drury Lane Theatre and ' late Professor of the Arts and Sciences in York-buildings ') and Rietti, with the idea of turning them into a place of entertainment. The opposition of the Royal Hospital and the promoters' lack of capital for such a costly undertaking delayed its realisation for some years. The property was then divided into thirty-six shares of £1,000 each, and the shareholders set about turning it into a place of public amusement. From time to time we shall hear of the sale of ' a thirty-sixth share,' or of the death of a shareholder. A considerable number of shares was held by Sir Thomas Robinson, who later became director of entertainments. Sir Thomas Robinson, M.P. – known sometimes as ' long Sir Thomas Robinson,' the ' Knight of the Woeful Countenance,' or ' Ranelagh's Maypole and Garden of Delights ' – was an amateur of the fine arts, particularly of architecture. In his young days – he was born in 1700 – he travelled extensively in Europe, and became an enthusiastic admirer of Palladio. When he returned he rebuilt the family mansion at Rokeby, built parts of Ember Court, Surrey, the Gothic Gateway at Bishop Auckland, and the bridge over the Tees at Rokeby, besides designing the west wing of Castle Howard for his wife's brother. He was extravagant and exuberant in speech as in architecture. As Member for the Borough of Morpeth in the first Parliament of George II, he made several fine, lengthy speeches, and he was noted for the profusion of

[1] ' . . . there can be little doubt that the building was designed by Christopher Wren.' (C. G. T. Dean : Lord Ranelagh's House in Chelsea).

his compliments in social intercourse. When Ranelagh opened he was already on his way to the Barbadoes, where he had been appointed Governor. His love of building got him into trouble, and in 1747 he was recalled. It was then that his close association with Ranelagh Gardens began.

Meanwhile in January, 1742, Londoners sufficiently leisured and curious to go as far as the village of Chelsea by the Thames could watch workmen busy on the erection of a curious structure, mostly of wood, in the gardens of Ranelagh House. Should sightseers have been in doubt as to the plan and purpose of the building operations, they had only to read the newspapers. The magnificent Temple being erected there would be ' inferior to few publick buildings in Europe. It is near twenty feet more in diameter than the Rotunda at Rome,[1] and covered with a most excellent contriv'd Roof. The Cieling will be painted by a prime Master with Stories adapted to the use of the Place.[2] The Terms that support the Cieling and the Trophies of Musick are wrought by a cunning Artist, and will be enrich'd with burnish'd gold. The Bases and Capitals of the Columns with their Entablatures, will be the same, and their Shafts are to represent Egyptian Marble . . . The Circus will be illuminated by a beautiful Set of Lustres.' The Proprietors had also engaged ' a choice Band of Musick, and the best of our English Singers,' and for the convenience of visitors to this magnificent temple, they planned to ' set up several Vehicles in Imitation of the French Diligences, that are to run from Ranelagh-House to Hyde-Park Corner, to Buckingham Gate and to Westminster-Abbey.' The idea of this ' noble Structure ' was originally Lacy's, the architect was William Jones, architect of the East India Company, and the builders were

---

[1] Its external diameter was 185 feet : internal 150 feet.
[2] The ceiling seems never to have been painted by the Prime Master ; prints of the finished building in 1751 show a sky-blue dome, but it is later described as being ' olive colour with a rainbow round the extremity.' See page 143. Later in the century, painted medallions appear.

C

Messrs. Timbrel and Spencer, ' whose abilities are too well-known to need any Enconium.' Ladies and Gentlemen who had already ' agreed to subscribe to the Amphi-theatrical Structure in Ranelagh Gardens at Chelsea ' were desired to pay their money as soon as possible to Messrs. Green and Amber, Bankers in the Strand ; there were thirty-six shares of £1,000 each. The Proprietors, further, made it clear that their entertainments were to be carried on ' with the greatest Decency and Order,' and that gaming would never be allowed indoors or in the Gardens.

Such were the preliminary plans for that Rotunda, round which England's rulers, artists and writers, as well as ' Persons of inferior Rank ' were to process for the next sixty years, talking of current politics, or scandal, or the latest war news, commenting on one another's clothes, and listening with more or less attention to the fashionable singers, accompanied by a choice band of music, performing works of the most eminent contemporary composers – from Mr. Handel, in the early days, to Dr. Haydn at the end of the century.

But the Rotunda was not to be the only attraction of the new place of entertainment. There were to be the formal gardens, with gravel walks shaded by elms and yews, ' a beautiful octagon grass plat,' ' ye great Walk leading to the Thames,' a circular Temple of Pan, Ranelagh-House itself to be used for certain entertainments and later connected with the Rotunda by a colonnade, a ' Bason,' reflecting in its waters the grand Amphitheatre itself and with a fountain in the centre, and above all a ' Canal,' in which was an island supporting what is sometimes described as a Chinese House and sometimes as a Venetian Temple. To twentieth-century eyes this piece of eighteenth-century *chinoiserie* has no particular resemblance to either, but it adds the final touch of fantasy and inconsequence to the masquerade scenes which were so often to be enacted in the gardens.

By March, public curiosity had become a nuisance. Sight-seers hindered the workmen, and some damage had been done to the fabric. Henceforth there was to be a shilling admission to all who were not subscribers, and no one would be admitted on Sundays. (This would keep away the rowdy apprentices and their like, who were only free on Sundays.)

* * *

The idea of such a place of summer amusement was not new ; the Proprietors of Ranelagh had been inspired by the success of Vauxhall and Marylebone Gardens, both of which relied to a great extent on the outdoor attractions of open-air music, refreshments and dancing, but both of which could transfer their entertainments indoors if necessary. Spring Gardens, Vauxhall, had been open to the public in the seventeenth century, but their true Pleasure Gardens career started in June, 1732, and was to outlast that of Ranelagh by many years. Marylebone, more countrified and less sophisticated, had opened in 1737, but closed in 1776. There were numerous lesser resorts around London, most of them offering musical entertainments of varying quality. Some of them possessed medicinal springs, such as Islington Spa (opened in 1733) and Sadlers Wells (which had been known since the end of the seventeenth century). Some of them were little more than tea-gardens, with bowls and skittles as their chief attractions. Some were frequented by the Gentry and Quality, others by the Cits and the rowdy apprentices, and some were described as hardly places ' where the unprotected Female could venture with Impunity.' These Gardens were usually open from Easter to August or September, and in the main were evening resorts, though public breakfasts were fashionable until stopped by law in 1752. Warwick Wroth describes sixty-four of these Gardens in his book, *London Pleasure Gardens of the Eighteenth Century*, which is the classic on this subject.

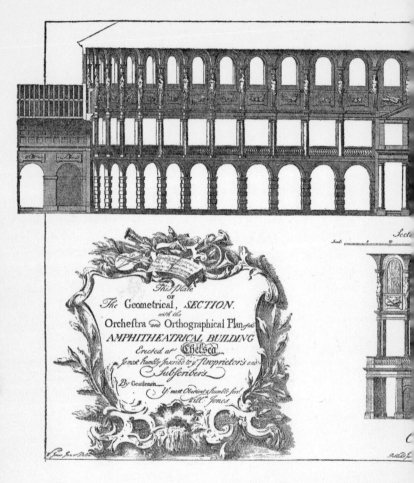

This Plate
OF
The Geometrical, SECTION.
with the
Orchestra and Orthographical Plan of the
AMPHITHEATRICAL BUILDING
Erected at Chelsea
Is most Humbly Inscrib'd to y.e Proprietor's and
Subscribers
By Gentlemen Y.r most Obedient & Humble Ser.t
Will.m Jones

A GEOMETRICAL SECTION

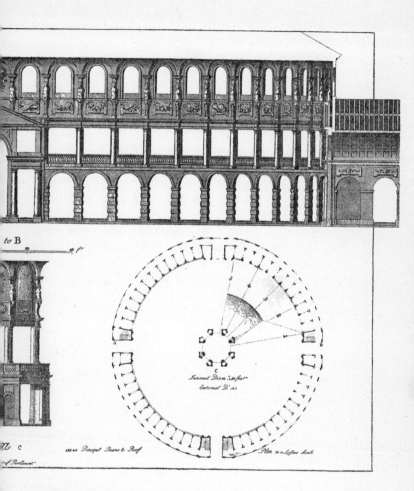

to B

Internal Diam. 140 feet
External D.º 185

132 to 2 Principal Beams to Roof

Plan to a Lesser Scale

OF THE ROTUNDA

One is sometimes tempted to imagine that English summers must have been more propitious to such outdoor amusements in the eighteenth century than in our own time. But we often read of fireworks spoilt with rain, and losses due to bad seasons. Horace Walpole thought the English summer was a fiction. 'People cry "This is a bad summer" – as if we ever had any other. The best sun we have is made of Newcastle coal, and I am determined never to reckon upon any other,' he wrote in June, 1768. Yet there were balmy evenings in those days as there are now, and eighteenth-century London provided many pleasant places in which to spend them. It can be said also that our taste in outdoor amusement has changed. The twentieth-century Londoner seems to prefer to take his fresh air while hitting a ball of some kind, whereas our ancestors' exercise was mainly confined to walking or riding, and they expected to be entertained rather than to exert themselves. On occasions such as Royal birthdays or peace celebrations, illuminations, fireworks and military reviews could be seen in the parks ; and wrestling matches between servants backed by their masters, or races between fat cooks and lean footmen, were among the more everyday spectacles. The English fondness for fresh air in all weathers was already conspicuous. Even as early as *The Tatler* we read that ' no frost, snow, nor east wind, can hinder a large set of people from going to the Park in February ; no dust or heat in June.'

It was the age not only of the Pleasure Gardens, but of the development of London's parks, in which Queen Caroline took a personal interest. It is to her we owe the Serpentine. Kensington Gardens was still royal, and Hyde Park was gradually coming into fashion as building spread westward, but ' The Park ' meant St. James's, which was in the centre of fashion. It was thronged every day before dinner, between twelve and two, and between seven and twelve on summer evenings. Queen Caroline once toyed with the idea of turning

' The Park ' back into a royal garden, and asked Sir Robert Walpole what the cost would be. ' Only three Crowns,' replied that Minister, who had done so much to give security to the somewhat shaky Hanoverian Crown. The Queen took the hint, and ' The Park ' remained the fashionable rendez-vous of which we read in memoirs and fiction all through the century. Pall Mall, too, was a favourite promenade.

* * *

The Thames meant more to Londoners of the eighteenth century than it does to us, and the fact that Cuper's Gardens, Vauxhall and Ranelagh had river frontages was one of their chief assets ; you could go to them by boat, instead of in a lumbering coach. The river was a busy thoroughfare on which could be seen sailing-boats, rowing-boats, with bright green or red seats, manned by watermen in white coats with red or blue breeches, and the barges of the nobility with their eighteen oars. Ranelagh regattas were a charming feature of its middle and late period, as will be seen hereafter, and the most gorge-ous spectacle ever seen on the Thames was probably the 1775 regatta. There were landing-places at frequent intervals along the river's banks, beside which boats could be tied up to long poles, like those in Venice.

From the City itself down to Kew and Richmond, each reach had its special charm and found a painter to record it. In Zoffany's conversation piece we see the Garricks entertain-ing Dr. Johnson at Hampton ; Devis shows us Horace Walpole presenting Kitty Clive with a piece of honeysuckle at Twicken-ham ; Samuel Scott gives us a river view of City spires and the dome of St. Paul's, with Somerset House in the foreground ; Canaletto paints not only the Rotunda at Ranelagh itself, but London and its river from the terrace of Richmond House ; from Thomas Moulton we gain an idea of what the Adelphi looked like from the river in 1797. Chelsea, Fulham, Chiswick,

Strand-on-the-Green, Kew, Twickenham, Hampton and Richmond were favourite spots for country cottages, and there were royal residences at Hampton Court, Richmond and Kew.

Music, specially that of French horns, was constantly heard on the river, and one of Ranelagh's first music-makings, a fore-taste of what was to come, took place many years before the foundations of the Rotunda were laid. On July 17th, 1717, Baron Kilmansegg gave a river concert to his master, King George I. The King got into his barge about eight o'clock, accompanied by the Duchess of Bolton and other members of the court. Beside the royal barge was a floating orchestra, a band of fifty instrumentalists (trumpets, horns, oboes, bas-soons, flutes and strings) which played a new suite of pieces by Mr. Handel as they proceeded up stream. Other barges, and boats filled with onlookers joined the procession. The King was so pleased with the music that he heard it twice through, once before and once after the splendid supper of which he partook at one in the morning at the house of the late Lord Ranelagh at Chelsea.

There are several water-music scenes in Horace Walpole's letters. For instance, there was the evening in June, 1748, when he watched from under the trees of Marble Hill ' Prince Lobkowitz's footmen in very rich new liveries, the two last bearing torches; and after them the Prince himself, in a new sky-blue watered tabby coat, with gold buttonholes, and a magni-ficent gold waistcoat fringed, leading Madame l'Ambassadrice de Venise in a green sack with a straw hat, attended by my Lady Tyrawley, Wall the private Spanish agent, the two Miss Molyneux's, and some other men. They went into one of the Prince of Wales's barges, had another barge filled with violins and hautboys, and an open boat with drums and trumpets.' There was ' the firework ' which the Duke of Richmond gave at his house at Whitehall in May, 1749. ' The garden lies with a slope down to the Thames, on which were lighters, from whence were thrown up, after a concert of water music, a great number of rockets. Then from boats on every side were water rockets and fires of that kind ; and then the wheels which were ranged along the rails of the terrace were played off . . . You can't conceive a prettier sight ; the garden filled with everybody of fashion.' And then there was an expedition to Vauxhall in 1750 when ' We got into the best order we could and marched to our barge, with a boat of French horns attending, and little Ashe singing. We paraded some time up the river, and at last debarked at Vauxhall.'

Music parties, such as that of the Sharps who lived at Fulham and were painted with their musical instruments in their shallop by Zoffany in 1781, must often have floated melodiously past Ranelagh Gardens.

* * ..

Indeed, when Ranelagh opened, the river was a pleasanter thoroughfare than the streets, whose pavements were inferior to those of most continental towns, and which, when narrow, were almost impassable on rainy days because of the water cascading from the projecting gutters. Nor was it only rain that was liable to descend upon passers-by ; the contents of homely domestic utensils were often emptied out of windows without warning. As the century went on, however, London streets became more cleanly. A measure had been introduced in 1736 to enable the Lord Mayor and Aldermen to erect glass lamps throughout London, and to keep them lighted from sunset to sunrise, which somewhat lessened the dangers to be apprehended from robbers and drunks. The protection afforded by the law against assaults in the streets was inadequate ; constables were recruited from the ranks of those too decrepit or physically weak to get their living in any other way. It was good to know how to defend yourself. When Dr. Johnson

D

had his handkerchief stolen by a pickpocket in Grosvenor Square, he hastened after the thief, overtook him, seized him by the collar, shook him violently, and gave him such a smack in the face that he knocked him off the pavement into the gutter.

If you went into the suburbs at night, it was best to go armed and in company, even if you went by coach. One of the drawbacks to Marylebone Gardens was their distance from the town, and moonlight nights were considered preferable for such expeditions. Ranelagh patrons were sometimes attacked by Gentlemen of the Road on their way home, as will be seen later, and the Proprietors provided a horse patrol for many years on the approach road. The King's Road was notorious for highwaymen.

The fashionable quarters of London when Ranelagh's dome was being built included Golden Square, Leicester Fields, Charing Cross (where Dr. Johnson said was the full tide of human existence) and, of course, St. James's. The nobility were beginning to move westwards ; Grosvenor Square, New Bond Street, the upper part of Piccadilly, and the greater part of Oxford Street itself, were built by the end of the first half of the century, but apart from Cavendish Square there were few houses north of Oxford Street, and most of the space between Grosvenor Square and Piccadilly was open ground until 1764. To the east, London stretched far into Whitechapel, Radcliffe Highway and Wapping. In the City the merchant classes still lived where they worked, and the old houses on London Bridge had not yet been pulled down.

*   *   *

The winter music of fashionable Londoners included the Italian opera, Mr. Handel's oratorios, some ballad operas – the fashion for which had been launched in 1728 with *The Beggar's Opera* – a few subscription concerts, and private music parties. Public concerts in the modern sense were unknown.

London's season was from October to May, and singers and other musicians migrated to the summer theatres or the Pleasure Gardens for the summer. The Pleasure Gardens, in particular, gave opportunities to English singers and song-writers which they would not find elsewhere.

Why was this ? Italian singers and methods of singing had begun to appear in English musical life as early as the time of Purcell, but they did not seriously challenge the English school till the beginning of the eighteenth century. From then onwards England was flooded with Italian opera and Italian opera-singers for many years. English singers held their own, however. Many of them mastered the Italian style, but at the same time a few composers preserved a distinctive style of English song, which required an English style of singing. The success of *The Beggar's Opera* and its many imitators, and the rise of Pleasure Gardens music were two important factors in the preservation of native song. The Italian *bel canto* meant the perfection of technique, in which the voice was used primarily as an instrument to produce sounds of sensuous beauty, and to perform vocal gymnastics of sensational virtuosity. English singing, on the other hand, had always laid great stress on the literary and dramatic aspects of song. The practical English soon tired of sounds, however beautiful, in which they could hear no sense, and demanded songs in their own language so written that the words could be distinctly heard. Such songs were turned out by the thousand at the Pleasure Gardens by composers of distinction, such as Dr. Arne, Dr. Boyce, and James Hook, and by the lesser fry. Yet the *bel canto* lived in the public taste, in spite of the ridicule poured upon its exaggerations, and the two kinds of singing – Italian and English – soon settled down and lived together peaceably. Some singers successfully practised both.

Frank Kidson went so far as to say that ' If we eliminate from the published music of the time all that had its first

Canaleti delin.

Publish'd according

An Inside View of the Rotundo in Ranelagh Gardens

Re-Publish'd 12ᵗʰ May. 1794 by I.AURE

Vue de l'Interieur de la Rotonde dans le Jardins de Ranelagh.

THE ROTUNDA

hearing at the public gardens, there would be very little left to
show what English music was like in the eighteenth century.'
Trivial some of these productions may have been, but they
seldom lack the very English quality of tunefulness and the
very eighteenth-century quality of elegance. We shall look in
vain for a seventeenth-century depth of feeling in either words
or music.   The Damons, the Strephons and the Colins, the
Hebes, the Sylvias and the Chloes tell the stories of their
pastoral loves in verses which invariably rhyme ' swain ' with
' plain ' and ' love ' with ' rove ' ; they milk cows, or tend
sheep in a genteel eighteenth-century manner, and do not take
anything too seriously. In appearance we imagine them something like the figures produced by the Porcelain Works at
Chelsea, not far from Ranelagh itself. There is often humour,
sometimes broad, but more often ironical, and these songs are
a long way from the sentimental Victorian ballad of a century
later. The poet of ' Platonic Love,' for instance (set to music by
Dr. Arne), frankly says that this is a form of the tender passion
for which he has no use, and he has certainly no intention of
dying of unrequited affection :—

> *In vain, my love, you bid me strive*
> *To keep a famished flame alive ;*
> *Unfed, the strongest flame won't burn,*
> *And love grows cold without return.*
>
> *The prude, perverse, or wither'd maid*
> *Whose ev'ry hope of love's decay'd,*
> *May flatter her despair to prove*
> *The illusions of platonic love.*

One of Dr. Boyce's heroines resolves to throw herself into the
Thames because she has been jilted, but decides against suicide after all, since she has ' but one life and there's a choice of
swains.' A young lady called Lucy, having vainly pursued her
fickle Strephon, decides that ' a man when we've got him is

scarce worth the pains.' The lyrics of these songs are not great poetry, but it was very important that their words should be distinctly heard, and this is where the English singers excelled. There were, too, topical songs about the fashions or the wars, which depended even more upon clear articulation for their effect. Musically, the best of these songs have the grace and decorative quality of the furniture, clothes, and silver of the period. Pieces of craftsmanship rather than works of art, perhaps, but it was the supreme age of craftsmanship.

* * *

Drama and Music were not the Londoners' only amusements. There were taverns, coffee-houses and clubs of all types for gentlemen. It was during Ranelagh's sixty years' reign that the Club as we know it to-day evolved. At the end of the seventeenth century ' clubs ' were established in Coffee Houses, Chocolate Houses or Taverns ; that is to say groups of men, bound together by some common interest, would engage a private room at some place of public entertainment. To take a famous instance, ' White's ' was originally a club which met at White's Chocolate House, opened at the end of the seventeenth century. By 1755 – after three moves and a fire – it seems to have become a Club in the modern sense, and as early as 1753 we hear that ' no person of what rank soever is admitted without first being proposed by one of the Club.' Gambling and betting both at Clubs such as White's and in private assemblies reached the highest pitch in eighteenth-century London. Cock-fighting was considered a manly and gentlemanly sport to watch, as Hogarth showed in 1759 and Rowlandson some sixty years later, and bear-baiting had not died out.

Drinking was heavy among all classes. In 1751 Hogarth's Gin Lane showed pictorially what Fielding described about the same time in his pamphlet *An Enquiry into the Causes of the Late Increase of Robbers Etc.*, namely, the appalling effect upon the working-classes of cheap spirits, often their only form of enjoyment. Other and more genteel kinds of drunkenness were taken as a matter of course.

It was indeed an age of contrasts. The same fashionable gentlemen who flocked to the opening of Ranelagh in their velvets and silks, who discoursed upon Taste so learnedly, and applauded the music of the best masters so genteelly, attended not only cock-fightings and bear-baitings, but also the frequent public executions at Tyburn. Temporary seats were erected upon a site belonging to the widow of a cowkeeper named Proctor, and the charge for ' Mother Proctor's Pews ' varied according to the importance of the criminal or criminals whose death was to be witnessed. Dr. Johnson himself approved of public executions and considered that if they did not draw spectators, they failed of their purpose. Hanging, indeed, might seem a better fate than mouldering in an eighteenth-century gaol, though transportation gave such of these wretches as survived the voyage a chance to make a new career and found respectable families in the colonies like New Jersey, Pennsylvania, the Carolinas, and Georgia. The American War of Independence put a stop to this form of colonisation, and offenders were huddled into convict galleys moored in the Thames, unless they were ' pressed ' for the army and navy, until the penal settlement of Botany Bay was founded. Masquerades and cock-fightings ; water-music and convict galleys ; songs about Damon and Phyllis, and the latest broadsheet with the True Confession of some thief just hanged at Tyburn ; the Gardens of Ranelagh, and Gin Lane ; the Rotunda, and Newgate – these all belonged to the same London, and need to be taken into account if we are to have a true picture of the whole.

*   *   *

But the violence of these contrasts can lead us astray. It would be to falsify the whole picture if we were to imagine

London neatly divided between elegant frivolity on the one hand and sordid misery or actual crime on the other. There were plenty of people in between the very rich and the very poor. Indeed, it was the age which saw the rise of a prosperous, self-respecting middle class, and an age of expanding commerce. There was also a steep rise in the population; the 5½ million of the reign of Queen Anne became 9 million in the reign of George III.

Although the contemporary accounts of Ranelagh festivities keep up the fiction of their being exclusively patronised by ' the Nobility and Gentry,' a large proportion of the promenaders belonged to the business and commercial classes. Anyone who could pay the usual admission money of 2s. 6d. was at liberty to come to Ranelagh's ordinary evenings, and though this was too high for the poorer people, it was well within the reach of the middle classes. As Sir John Fielding said, Ranelagh and Vauxhall were not entirely appropriated to ' the people of fashion,' though they were ' seldom frequented by any below middle rank.' No one was turned out of Ranelagh except for ill-behaviour.

A Circumstantial Account of the Regatta (see Chapter IV) has something to say on this subject : ' Public spectacles in a free country should be exhibited at as moderate an expence as elegance and decency will permit ; and should be so contrived that the middle rank of society may inoffensively be admitted to partake of those diversions, as well as those of the first fashion. By this means a dignity is maintained in every class of the community, and a degree of politeness diffuses itself through the several orders of the spectators.'

All through the century there was a progressive levelling of classes, and in 1784 the *European Magazine* wrote that ' all sorts of people are frequently confounded or melted down into one glaring mass of superfluity or absurdity. The lower classes are entirely lost in a general propensity to mimic the

E

finery of the higher.' The self-made man might serve in
Parliament or be raised to the peerage, and a new aristocracy of
wealth was growing up, composed of nabobs, planters,
bankers, merchants and manufacturers. There were, too, the
large professional classes – the lawyers, the doctors, and the
literary gentlemen – all of whom were as well represented
among the promenaders in the Rotunda as were the old
aristocracy, the new plutocracy, and the landed gentry.

*   *   *

What was the world position of this London and this
England when Ranelagh first opened ?

1742 marks the end of that long period of peace-at-all-costs,
which the great Whig leader, Sir Robert Walpole, had ensured
for the nation. It had enabled him to consolidate the work of
the 1688 Revolution, to establish the Hanoverian dynasty
firmly on the throne, and to develop the Cabinet system of
government. His true partner in this work had been not
George II, but George II's far-seeing and long-suffering con-
sort, Queen Caroline. The Hanoverian royal family enjoyed
little personal popularity or affection until the accession of the
British-born George III, Farmer George, in 1760, long after
Sir Robert's day. Even Horace Walpole, a Whig of the Whigs,
spoke of them as ' Messieurs les Allemands.' But they were
the lesser of two evils, and most moderate men felt that ' the
Protestant succession ' meant stability and security. 1739 was
the beginning of the end of Walpole's age ; a dispute over the
trading monopoly with Spanish America involved us in war
with both Bourbon powers, Spain and France. Walpole
retained office, though he disapproved of the war – ' It is your
war,' he said to Newcastle, ' and I wish you joy of it ' – until
February, 1742, when he was defeated in the Commons,
became Lord Orford, and ceased to be a Minister of the
Crown. It was in that month of February, too, while Ranelagh

Gardens echoed to the hammers of workmen, that the term
Prime Minister was first used.

Ranelagh and the new age were born together. It was to be
an age of imperial expansion and European commitments, and
the topic of war – whether on the Continent, in India, in
Canada or in America, at sea or on land – was never to be long
absent from the conversations of the promenaders in the
Rotunda and its Gardens. It even crept into the music. The
bogy of France, whether represented by the Bourbons, the
Revolution, or Bonaparte, was only to be exorcised for brief
intervals.

The Rotundo, Houf

London printed for te

RANELAGH HO

Gardens, &c. at Ranelagh.

at the Golden Buck in Fleet Street.

OTUNDA AND GARDENS

I

1742 – 1747

THE SECOND SILESIAN WAR

ALTHOUGH Ranelagh's official opening was April 5th, 1742, Horace Walpole wrote to Sir Horace Mann on April 15th that the building was not yet finished. He had breakfasted there that morning, and reported that they ' had built an immense amphitheatre, with balconies full of little alehouses ; it is in rivalry to Vauxhall, and cost about twelve thousand pounds . . . they get great sums by people going to see it and break-fasting in the house [*i.e.*, presumably Ranelagh House, since the Rotunda was not yet completed] : there were yesterday no less than three hundred and eighty persons, at eighteen pence a piece. You see how poor we are, when, with a tax of four shillings in the pound, we are laying out such sums for cakes and ale.' (Later, and during most of its history, admission was to be 2s. 6d., which included tea or coffee.) The neighbour-hood was familiar to him, for as a boy he had lived hard by at Walpole House. On May 26th he had more to say about Rane-lagh, which had been opened again two nights previously, when the Prince and Princess of Wales, the Duke, ' much

nobility and much mob were there.' Into ' the vast amphitheatre, finely gilt, painted and illuminated,' everybody ' that
loves eating, drinking, staring or crowding is admitted for
twelve pence,' while twice a week there are to be ridottos with
tickets price one guinea, which would include supper and
music.

Even when not in masquerade, the costumes of the Ranelagh ' nobility and mob ' that season would seem sufficiently
gay to our eyes. It was the age of the *sacque* gown for women
which hung loose from the shoulders and spread over the bell-
shaped hooped petticoat, which was often hand-embroidered
in a floral pattern ; on the petticoat of one court costume in the
year 1741, for instance, were embroidered ' brown hills
covered with all sorts of weeds, and every breadth had an old
stump of a tree that run up almost to the top of the petticoat
round which twined nasturtions, ivy, honeysuckle, peri-
winkles, convolvuses, and all sorts of twining flowers which
spread and covered the petticoat.' Bodices were cut low, and
sometimes filled in with soft fichus of lace or muslin, and lace
fell over the wrists. Hair was worn close to the head, and
curled, usually under a cap, which might be very elaborate.
Ladies who visited Ranelagh Gardens in the daytime were
fond of wearing straw hats, tied under the chin with ribbon,
for there was a fashion for the pseudo-pastoral in dress as in
song. (During its sixty years, the Rotunda was to see many
changes in the feminine silhouette.) Floral embroidery
appeared on the gentlemen's waistcoats also that season, and
the stuffs they wore were no less rich than those of their ladies.
Wigs were small, though an old gentleman might cling to his
full-bottomed wig from conservatism. Shoe-buckles, waistcoat buttons, and the ladies' jewellery sparkled in the candle-
light.

Horace Walpole himself was conservative in his tastes, and
still preferred Vauxhall, when the weather inclined him to

think of al fresco entertainment. But on the whole, he liked his own fireside or the theatre better. At Drury Lane, Kitty Clive had been very amusing in a new farce, and John Beard – later to be one of Ranelagh's most famous singers – not so amusing. And there was another new attraction in the London of 1742. Everyone was running to Goodman's Fields to see a wine merchant of the name of Garrick who had turned player ; he ' plays all parts, and is a very good mimic,' but Horace saw nothing wonderful in it.

George II took a fancy to Ranelagh, and pressed people to go to its entertainments ; he was very fond of masquerades, and enjoyed one in July from a box decked with red which effectually prevented his remaining incognito, while ' an hundred men, six women and two shepherdesses ' amused themselves in the Rotunda and Gardens. Horace Walpole was rather bored. (' Masquerade ' or ' Ridotto ' will be found used throughout the century to describe the same form of entertainment. George II's Swiss Master of the Revels, Heidegger, had been largely responsible for popularising masquerades at the Opera House in the Haymarket, enthusiastically supported by his royal master. But there was an outcry against the immorality of this amusement ; the Bishop of London preached against it at Bow Church in 1726 before the Society for the Reformation of Manners, and in 1729 a Middlesex Grand Jury described Heidegger as ' the principal promoter of vice and immorality.' The chief result of this outcry was that masquerades went on as before, under the name of ridottos.)

A French visitor described his impressions of a Ranelagh evening in 1742 in the *Gentleman's Magazine* :' I repaired to the rendezvous which was the park adjoining to the Palace Royal [*i.e.*, St. James's Park] . . . where we sauntered with a handful of company until it was almost twilight – a time I thought a little unseasonable for a tour into the country. We had no sooner quitted the park but we found ourselves in a road full of people, illuminated with lamps on each side ; the dust was the only inconvenience ; but in less than half an hour we found ourselves at a gate where money was demanded.'

There were two routes for carriages, from Hyde Park Corner or from Buckingham Gate, and people who chose to walk usually went through St. James's Park to Buckingham Gate, as did our French friend, and then followed the well-lighted thoroughfare for three-quarters of a mile.

He went on : ' Immediately my eyes were struck with a large building of orbicular figure, with a row of windows round the attic story, through which it seemed to be liberally illuminated within, and altogether presented to the eye such an image as a man of whimsical imagination would not scruple to call a giant's lanthorn. Into this enchanted palace we entered, I, for my part, found myself dumb with surprise and astonishment, in the middle of a vast amphitheatre ; for structure, Roman ; for decorations of paint and gilding, gay as the Asiatic ; four grand portals, in the manner of the ancient triumphal arches, and four times twelve boxes, in a double row, with suitable pilasters between, form the whole interior of this wonderful fabric, save that in the middle a magnificent orchestra rises to the roof, from which descend several large branches, which contain a great number of candles enclosed in crystal glasses . . . Groups of well-dressed persons were dispersed in the boxes, numbers covered the area ; all manner of refreshments were within call ; and music of all kinds echoed, though not intelligibly, from every one of those elegant retreats, where Pleasure seemed to beckon her wanton followers.'

The last sentence seems to imply that the ladies and gentlemen gossiping and flirting in the boxes were making their own music, but our foreign visitor admits that his eyes were dazzled and his head giddy, so perhaps his ears were also deceived. Amateur music may have been produced by the wanton followers of Pleasure in these elegant retreats, but the professional music came from the centre of the building, where a ' grand and elegant structure ' supported the roof and contained the orchestra in those early days. After a few years, the orchestra was moved to the side of the Rotunda.

On June 1st, 1742, Mrs. Elizabeth Carter described the Rotunda as follows : ' To untravelled eyes, like mine, 'tis, to be sure, an amazing fine thing, and quite worthy of your coming to town to see it next year, by which time they may possibly have found all that it wants to make it complete, and some use for it answerable to the fineness and stateliness of the structure, for, to be sure, it is quite vexatious at present to see all the pomp and splendour of a Roman amphitheatre devoted to no better use than a twelvepenny entertainment of cold ham and chicken.'

It was not till the summer of 1743 that the battle of Ranelagh was truly won. (That summer another battle was won, that of Dettingen, at which one of Ranelagh's first patrons, George II, commanded his forces in person.) Ranelagh was open at six o'clock in the evening on Wednesday and Friday that season, and the 2s. 6d. admission fee included tea and coffee.

By 1744 even Horace Walpole had succumbed to its charms, and writes that it ' has totally beat Vauxhall. Nobody goes anywhere else – everybody goes there. My Lord Chesterfield is so fond of it, that he says he has ordered all his letters to be directed thither. If you had never seen it, I would make you a most pompous description of it, and tell you how the floor is all of beaten princes – that you can't set your foot without treading on a Prince of Wales or Duke of Cumberland. The company is universal ; there is from his Grace of Grafton down to Children out of the Foundling Hospital – from my Lady Townshend to the kitten.'

The 1744 season opened almost simultaneously with the

Second Silesian War. On March 31st war had been declared against France, for having violated the Pragmatic Sanction, assisted Spain against England, and lent help to Prince Charles Edward, son of the Stuart claimant to the throne. Sir Robert Walpole, now Lord Orford, prophesied that this new war policy would bring danger to the Hanoverian dynasty which he had given the best part of his life to establish. But his was a voice from the past, the voice of a dying man. His prophecy of an attack on the dynasty was to be fulfilled the next year, when he himself was in his grave. But his work had not been in vain. The attack failed, and the Hanoverian dynasty survived.

England was now fairly launched on a new path, and Ranelagh on its sixty years' career of fashion.

*   *   *

In the first years the Band of Music was led by Michael Christian Festing, who was an eminent violinist of the period, member of the King's private band, first violin of the Philharmonic Society which met at the Crown and Anchor, director of the Italian opera, one of the founders of the Society of Musicians, and a soloist at every benefit concert of importance. Compared with the violinists of the end of the century, such as Cramer, Barthelemon and Pieltain, he seems to have been no great performer ; Burney says he had ' a feeble hand, little genius for composition, and but a shallow knowledge of counterpoint.' But in his day he held a unique position, until he was superseded by Giardini. Whether he was the son of a flautist of the same name who played in the King's Theatre Orchestra, or of a German-born aide-de-camp to Prince Eugene, killed at the battle of Blenheim, seems difficult to determine ; the evidence for the latter hypothesis rests partly on a statement in the unreliable *Georgian Era*, and partly on an unsigned manuscript, which alleges that the Duke of Marlborough brought forward both Michael Christian and his brother John, a flautist and oboist, out of regard for their dead father. John also did very well in the musical world, particularly as a teacher of the flute. Apart from the respect which his musical talents inspired, Michael Christian Festing was noted for the integrity of his character, and what Burney calls his ' gentlemanlike behaviour,' at a time when gentleman-like behaviour was sufficiently unusual in musicians to call for comment.

Among the singers the first season was Mr. Sullivan, whom Mrs. Delany was to describe some years later as ' a *block* with a very fine voice,' when he sang in the first performance of Handel's *Joseph*. He had sung with Mr. and Mrs. Lampe at Chester in 1741, and was to be the first singer of ' God Save the King ' at Bath in November, 1745.

*   *   *

Two months before Mr. Sullivan introduced ' God Save the King ' to Bath, the audience at the Theatre Royal in Drury Lane had been ' agreeably surpriz'd by the Gentlemen belonging to that House performing the Anthem of God Save our noble King.' That was on September 28th, but the words

> *Confound the enemies*
> *Of George our King !*

expressed the sentiments of all sensible people during the preceding summer, even of those who had no great love for George II. Who would wish to exchange the Hanoverian Succession (unattractive though its present representative might be) for the Stuarts, whose victory would mean domination by the French and the Papists ? Only declared Jacobites (and they were fighting for their Prince) could hold any other opinion. Whigs and Tories formed a common front against ' the despotick Attempts of Papal Power.' The chief difference between Whigs and Tories at that critical moment was that the

Whigs considered the danger largely due to our having abandoned Walpole's policy and thus entangled ourselves in a European war, while the Tories blamed the Whigs for not having prepared for that war during Walpole's long reign of peace.

Walpole himself did not live to see Prince Charlie's landing in the Hebrides, the Jacobite rising, or the final defeat of the Stuarts. But his son Horace (if he were indeed his son) wrote during Ranelagh's third season a day-to-day account of London's reactions to the war and the invasion, and his news and views were probably typical of those canvassed in the Rotunda that summer.

' It is quite the fashion to talk of the French coming here,' he wrote at the height of the Ranelagh season, ' Nobody sees it in any other light but as a thing to be talked of, not to be precautioned against . . . You see I laugh about it, for I would not for the world be so un-English as to do otherwise. I am persuaded that when Count Saxe, with ten thousand men, is within a day's march of London, people will be hiring windows at Charing Cross and Cheapside to see them pass by. 'Tis our characteristic to take dangers for sights, and evils for curiosities.'

Count Saxe never came within a day's march of London, or even landed on these shores, but in July Charles Stuart raised the standard of the White Rose at Glenfinnan, and by December the ' rebels ' were in Derby. The turn of the year brought the turn of the tide however, and by the time Ranelagh was opened in 1746 the danger was passed. On April 16th Culloden was fought, and as spring and summer went by promenaders in the Rotunda heard of the final defeat of the Rebellion, the capture of notable rebels, and the continued escape of The Boy himself.

*　　　*　　　*

During the month of June, Westminster Hall was being prepared for the trial of the Rebel Lords, while two miles

away Ranelagh gave a special masquerade for the Prince of
Hesse who was visiting London. This will not be the last time
we shall hear of a *cause célèbre* at Westminster Hall rivalling the
attractions of Ranelagh, but the trials later in the century are
not so melancholy as this one. Horace Walpole wrote a circumstantial account of the proceedings to his friend Horace Mann
at Florence, and though he was not at the execution of Lord
Kilmarnock and Lord Balmerino at the Tower of London, he
took care to have an account from two eye-witnesses. And of
course he went to see the newly-severed heads set up on
Temple Bar. Spy-glasses were let out at a halfpenny a look.
Soon there would be more heads, for the trials were not yet
over.

Meanwhile Michael Festing and his band of music performed at Ranelagh, with Parry the Welsh harper. John Parry
of Ruabon was Bard to Sir W. W. Wynne during the middle of
the eighteenth century, and also played in London. He died at
his native place in 1782. An organ was erected in the Rotunda
that season, with Keeble as its first organist. Keeble sometimes
played at St. George's, Hanover Square, when Roseingrave
was suffering from one of his periodic fits of insanity, and was
a fine organist. Butler later succeeded him at Ranelagh.

Lord Cholmondeley, who had borrowed money with some
difficulty to decorate his fine room at Richmond with damask,
thought himself insulted by a flowerseller at the gates of Ranelagh, when she offered him roses with the commendation
' Right damask, my Lord ! ' ; while Thomas Gray spent his
evenings at Vauxhall or Ranelagh, and the rest of his time with
Horace Walpole in Arlington Street or at ' the Tryal of the
Lords.' In August the Duke of Cumberland was back from his
victories and his brutalities in Scotland, staying at Cumberland Lodge ' with three whores and three aide-de-camps.' But
by September the season was over, which was wretched for
Horace Walpole, who was showing London to an Italian

marquis and found ' not a soul in town ; no plays, and Ranelagh shut up.'

*　　*　　*

When the spring season of 1747 began, sky-rockets and fireworks were celebrating in retrospect the victory of Culloden,
and Mr. Handel had just produced *Judas Maccabæus* at
Covent Garden, dedicated to ' a truly wise, valiant and virtuous commander,' that same Duke of Cumberland. There were
more heads on Temple Bar, and in March Horace Walpole had
' lived at ' the trial of Simon, Lord Lovat.

Meanwhile, the country was heartily sick of the war with
France which was a long way off, and had begun with no
adequate cause, or so it now seemed. Hawke and Anson beat
the French at sea, but the truly wise, valiant and virtuous commander was less successful in Flanders than he had been in the
Highlands. In fact, ' we were beat on every spot in which my
Lord Marlborough had conquered.' London was very empty
that summer, and not very cheerful.

II

1748 – 1756

BETWEEN TWO WARS

BUT by the opening of the 1748 season, preliminaries of peace had been signed, stocks had risen, and everyone was feeling happier. Now that there was peace in Europe there was time for the promenaders in the Rotunda to think and talk of those colonies in the East and West Indies, and in North America which were becoming more and more important. Money could be made out of them, new commodities came from them, and a gentleman might obtain a secretaryship in some remote place such as Jamaica or Barbados, which he could profitably farm out to a deputy if he did not want to exile himself. Had not Ranelagh's Sir Thomas Robinson been Governor of the Barbados for nearly five years ? and George Selwyn, that great wit and connoisseur of executions, was Registrar to the Court of Chancery in Barbados, but never even visited the island. A younger son might do worse than become collector of taxes in, say, North Carolina. Sugar-planters made fortunes in the West Indies, and everyone knew that the East Indies were an El Dorado ; the nabobs' wives who paraded at Ranelagh were plastered with diamonds. In fact, if we must fight wars, would it not be better to fight them to increase or preserve these same colonies than to intervene in some European dynastic squabble out of which we got nothing ? There were those who thought it a pity the King of England should also be Elector of Hanover, and should be so fond of the country of his birth, thus involving us in continental politics. As usual, he had gone to Hanover that summer, taking with him his fat German mistress, the Countess of Yarmouth.

Ranelagh was very crowded. One evening there was a traffic block which held up coaches for thirty-six minutes, and inside the Rotunda the fashionable ladies were almost hoop to hoop.

*   *   *

The peace celebrations waited until the end of April, 1749, when the town was illuminated, and in July Ranelagh produced a ' Jubilee Masquerade in the Venetian Manner,' at the request of the masquerade-loving king. (It was said his German mistress had persuaded him to patronise Ranelagh in this way, because one of her compatriots was a shareholder.) His Majesty attended in person, as well as the Prince and Princess of Wales, and the Duke of Cumberland.

The Gardens were dotted with tents, and here and there were bands of martial music – French horns, kettledrums, etc. – masked, and dressed as peasants or huntsmen. There was a maypole, round which danced more masks to the music of pipe and tabor, which seems strangely un-Venetian. But on the canal was another band of music in a gondola, and all round the outside of the Rotunda were shops in imitation of those in the Piazza at Venice. The amphitheatre itself was 'elegantly illuminated,' and adorned with fir-trees 20 – 30 feet high (do fir-trees grow in Venice ?), orange trees with small lamps in each artificial orange, auriculas in pots, and festoons of natural flowers. It pleased Horace Walpole more than

G

anything he ever saw. There was 'a genteel collation,' tea, wine, dancing to ' proper music,' and, contrary to the promise made by the Proprietors in 1742, booths for gaming.

* * *

During the course of the evening John Beard sang a topical song of which the composer remains deservedly anonymous. Here are two specimen verses of the words :—

Tho' our revels are scorn'd by the grave and the wise,
Yet they practise all day what they seem to despise ;
Examine mankind from the great to the small,
Each mortal's disguis'd, and the world is a ball.

Sing tantarara masks all.

The Parson brimful of October *and grace,*
With a long taper pipe and a round ruddy face,
Will rail at our doings—but when it is dark,
The Doctor's disguis'd, and led home by the Clerk.

Sing tantarara masks all.

* * *

English tenors should regard John Beard as their patron saint, the founder of their race. It was Mr. Handel who first put tenors on the musical map, and John Beard was Handel's first tenor. Tenor voices existed, of course, before his day, but were relegated to minor parts in the early days of Italian opera, when the hero was always performed by a powerful castrato soprano (or even contralto). Whether Handel was tired of the castrato type of voice and singing, or only tired of the pretensions and ' temperaments ' of these expensive and adulated creatures, and thought tenors would be both cheaper and easier to manage, it is difficult to decide. If the latter was his reason for writing leading parts for tenors, he made a serious

Myrtilla

Sung by Mr Beard at Ranelagh.

Siciliana

Ye Chearful Virgins have ye feen my fair Myrtilla pafs the Green to Rofe or Jefmine Bow'r To Rofe or Jefmine Bow'r Where does fhe feek the Woodbine Shade for fure ye know the blooming Maid Sweet as the May born Flow'r Sweet Sweet as the May born Flow'r.

2

Her Cheeks is like the Maiden Rofe,
Join'd with the Lilly as it blows,
Where each in fweetnefs vie,
Like dew drops gliftning in the Morn,
When Phœbus gilds the Flow'ring Thorn,
Health fparkles in her Eye.

3

Her Song is like the Linnets Lay,
That warbles chearful on the Spray,
To hail the Vernal Beam,
Her Heart is blyther than her Song,
Her Pafsions gently move along,
Like the fmooth gliding Stream.

For the Flute

mistake, which he did not live long enough to find out, for tenors in his day had not yet learnt their power, and do not seem to have been harder to manage than basses; perhaps they were still too surprised to find themselves in the position of principals to think of aping the manners of their predecessors.

John Beard was born about 1716, and educated at the Chapel Royal under Gates, where as a boy he sang the Israelitish Priest in the performance of *Esther* given by Gates to Handel as a birthday treat in 1732. Handel was impressed by his grown-up voice, and promised he would ' surprise the Town with his Performance.' Beard made his debut as a Handelian tenor in *Alexander's Feast* on February 19th, 1736, and was subsequently associated with nearly all the oratorios. Pencillings on the manuscript scores show that Handel had his voice in mind when writing many of his tenor parts. He sang also at the theatres and Pleasure Gardens.

There are many tributes to the uprightness and amiability of his character, but in 1739 he committed a grave error ; he, a singer, married Lady Harriet Herbert, widow of Colonel Herbert and only daughter of Lord Waldegrave. The teatables were, as usual, more severe on the lady than on the man (gentleman he could scarcely be called). It was thought that she might just as well have married her lackey, and Lady Mary Wortley Montagu thought such examples ' detrimental to the whole sex.' After fourteen years of what was apparently a happy marriage, the erring Lady Harriet died, and, as his second wife, Beard married a daughter of John Rich of Covent Garden – undoubtedly a more suitable match – and on the death of his father-in-law became part-owner of the theatre. It was he who courageously resisted the Half Price Rioters in 1763. He last appeared in 1767 in *Love in a Village*, and died at Hampton Court in 1791.

But all that was far in the future in the year 1749, when he was still married to Lady Harriet, and probably the most popular singer of the day. His voice seems to have been more powerful than sweet, but a natural male voice and an intelligent delivery must have made a special appeal to a public which had heard so much sensuous beauty of tone and so many studied graces. Walpole says he had only one note to his voice, but admits that he ' did more justice to sense than any of our performers.' He was, in fact, an English singer, and well-suited to singing Pleasure Gardens ballads, as well as Handelian airs. But though an English singer, he had enough of the flexibility of the Italians to be able to execute the most difficult divisions. One of his most popular Ranelagh songs was Dr. Boyce's *The Non Pareil* (' Tho' Chloe's out of fashion ').

* * *

It was at another masquerade during that gay summer of 1749 that Elizabeth Chudleigh, Maid of Honour to the Princess of Wales, shocked the town by her impersonation of Iphigenia, in draperies so scanty as to suggest Andromeda. A few years later her trial for bigamy was to be one of the many counter-attractions to Ranelagh which Westminster Hall provided in the course of the century. Iphigenia was now twenty-nine – famous for her charm, her freedom of manners, and her indelicacy, an eighteenth-century expression for which it is hard to find a twentieth-century equivalent. In truth, she was no longer Elizabeth Chudleigh, and had no real right to remain a Maid of Honour, for she had secretly married the Hon. Augustus John Hervey, Lieutenant in His Majesty's Navy, five years before at Lainston in Hampshire. As he was a younger son, dependent on his pay and prize money, the bride determined not to acknowledge her marriage for fear of losing the £400 per annum which her place at Court gave her. Two years before her appearance in the character of Iphigenia she had given birth to a child which was baptised at Old Chelsea Church and put out to nurse somewhere in the village, where it shortly died. Ann Cradock, her maid and confidant, afterwards testified that the child's death was a great grief to her lady, and one day when they were ' airing in the coach in Chelsea, she told her the child was buried there.' Indeed, the neighbourhood of Chelsea had some importance in the life of Iphigenia, for her father had been Deputy Governor of Chelsea College, and as a child she had played with little Horace Walpole very close to the Gardens of Ranelagh. (Sir Robert Walpole lived at Chelsea in Horace's young days.)

If Thackeray drew upon Elizabeth Chudleigh's career and character for Beatrice Esmond, he left plenty of material unused which other novelists might profit by, but it may be doubted if any fiction could improve upon the plain tale of her life. In 1749, her more notorious exploits lay in the future. Echoes of them will be heard beneath the Rotunda's dome from time to time.

*   *   *

Newspapers, letters and memoirs of these years give the impression that London life was one long *bal masqué*, illuminated by elegant fireworks, and moving to the tempo of Mr. Handel's music. Yet there were still many people who were shocked by masquerades and suchlike dissipations. Wesley and Whitfield were already preaching, and making converts not only among the poor but among that class that promenaded in the Rotunda. The sceptical Horace Walpole did not view these conversions with much sympathy, and wrote that ' the sect increases as fast as almost ever any religious nonsense did.'

But the new ' Enthusiasm ' was already shaking both the latitudinarianism and the scepticism which were equally typical of the eighteenth-century attitude to religion. And when earthquakes were felt in London in February and March 1750, they were thought by many to be a judgment on the frivolities of the age, especially on such diversions as Ranelagh masquerades. Because the March shock was felt exactly a month after that of February, a third was expected on April 5th, and many families evacuated to the country. Within three days, 730 coaches were counted passing Hyde Park Corner on their way to the innocent countryside, which was apparently considered outside the range of the wrath of God. Just as the ladies of 1940 made themselves Siren Suits, so did the ladies of 1750 make themselves warm Earthquake Gowns, in which they could sit up all night out of doors without catching cold.

The third earthquake did not come, and consciences soon recovered from the jolt which had been given them, but masquerades fell out of fashion for a brief period. (Scenes in Fielding's *Amelia* and other novels of the period, and Hogarth's *Ill Effects of Masquerades* show that the accusations made in the 20's of the century were not entirely out of date.) Instead, ' Balls after the Venetian Manner ' or ' after the Manner of the Jubilee ' were given at Ranelagh. (' Tickets price one guinea, to be delivered at White's Chocolate House in St. James's Street, and at Ranelagh, and nowhere else.') John Beard was still singing at Ranelagh, and that season we hear of one of the Scots songs which were to be popular for many years. Most of these later songs were manufactured in England, decorated with a few supposedly Scots words and plentifully sprinkled with the Scotch Snap (a semiquaver followed by a dotted quaver, which admittedly forms part of the strathspey rhythm). But 'The Highland Laddie,' 'written long since by Allan Ramsay, and now sung at Ranelagh and all the other Gardens, often fondly encored and sometimes ridiculously " hiss'd," ' seems to have been the genuine article. Concerts were frequently in the morning at this period, followed by a ' public breakfast,' which was included in the price of admission.

Indeed, it was safer to go into the outlying villages by day than by night. The disbanding of so many soldiers after the peace, combined with the ever-present evil of gin-drinking, had led to increased lawlessness and robberies. The Proprietors of Ranelagh promised ' a sufficient Guard within and without the House and Gardens, to prevent any Disorders or Indecencies, and to oblige Persons guilty immediately to quit the Place.' There was likewise a Guard on the roads. One Tuesday night between ten and eleven Mr. Talbot's coach returning from Ranelagh was stopped near Grosvenor Gate in Hyde Park by two well-mounted highwaymen in White Venetian masks who showed their pistols and then concealed them, for fear of frightening the ladies. The Gentlemen of the Road behaved, indeed, ' very civilly,' but took about twenty guineas and a gold watch in a studded case. Horace Walpole was sitting in his dining-room in Arlington Street one Sunday night just before eleven, when he heard a loud cry of ' Stop thief.' A highwayman had attacked a post-chaise in Piccadilly, and escaped.

Newgate Gaol was filled with the refuse of the disbanded army and navy, and so rife was gaol fever as a result of overcrowding and a lack of the most elementary forms of hygiene that the Lord Chief Justice considered it would be dangerous for persons to attend the business of the sessions at the Old Bailey ; twenty gentlemen had died as a result of malignant fevers contracted at the last sessions. John Howard had already begun his humanitarian work in prisons, and the need for reform was a crying one.

It was in January, 1751, that Henry Fielding published his *Enquiry into the Late Increase of Robbers*, ascribing the evil to ' a new kind of drunkenness unknown to our ancestors,' caused by the cheapness of gin ; the poorer classes could be ' drunk for a penny, dead drunk for tuppence.' In February of the same year Hogarth's ' Beer Street ' and ' Gin Lane ' appeared showing the good humour and prosperity which came from drinking wholesome beer, and the degradation and misery brought about by gin-drinking. The polite ladies and gentlemen who frequented Ranelagh were served with nothing so vulgar as beer or gin ; they drank tea or coffee in the Rotunda, or ' choice wines,' of which French claret, sherry, Marsala and port were the chief. The chairmen who bore them to Ranelagh in their sedan chairs and the strong porters who carried heavy bales of goods favoured a special brand of light ale which came to be known as ' Porter.' In their own homes, gentlemen drank one another under the table nightly and were carried up to bed by their servants, but at Ranelagh their conduct was strictly decorous.

In this year were published ' Seven Views of the most agreeable Parts of Vauxhall and Ranelagh Gardens,' engraved by ' the best Hands, from drawings made on the Spot, by Mr. Wale, Morier &c. Price 1s plain and 2s coloured.' They could be seen at ' Thomas Bowles in St. Paul's Church Yard, John Bowles at the Black Horse in Cornhill, Samuel Okey under St. Dunstan's Church, and Mrs. Chapel's in Grosvenor Street.' The Ranelagh views show ' The Rotunda with the Jubilee Ball,' ' The Chinese House and Garden, with the Company in Masquerade Habits,' and the ' Inside of the Rotunda with the Company at Breakfast.' Among the Masquerade Habits we can see nothing so startling as Miss Chudleigh's Iphigenia. There are a lady and gentleman in Scots costume, or what passed as such, a nun or so, some shepherdesses, some bishops, a Pope, while round the maypole dance a chinaman and figures from the *commedia dell'arte*. The everyday costumes of the ladies and gentlemen in the other views are to twentieth-century eyes fully as decorative as the Masquerade Habits. Ladies' hoops are wider and flatter, less bell-like in outline, than they were when the Gardens first opened ; over side panniers fall gowns which are perhaps of lawn or muslin, patterned with sprigs of flowers. Colours are clear and bright, and stuffs less rich and heavy than earlier in the century. Waists are small, bodices are still cut very low, and

H

ladies' hair is still dressed close to the head. A little cape sometimes covers the shoulders. Gentlemen's wigs are of reasonable size and their three-cornered hats not exaggeratedly small
or exaggeratedly large. Ladies carry fans. Gentlemen wear
swords, and carry canes. Such children as are to be seen are
miniature replicas of their parents.

The world of Ranelagh, as depicted in these views, seems
entirely remote from both Beer Street and Gin Lane. Yet all
three belonged to the same London of the year 1751, the year
in which Frederick Prince of Wales died, leaving as heir to the
throne a boy of thirteen.

That year the singers were John Beard, Giulia, Frasi and
Mrs. Storer. Frasi was a Handelian singer like Beard, and from
1749 onwards she sang regularly in his oratorios, singing also
in Italian opera. Her singing must have been ' Italian ' in
technique ; her smooth, chaste style is praised, but there are
complaints of her lack of feeling. Handel coached her in his
own works, and Burney, who often accompanied her, has
some anecdotes of their studies together. Once Handel brought
to Frasi's house the duet from *Judas Maccabæus*, which she
had not sung for two years, and sat down at the harpsichord,
expecting Burney to hum the lower part while he sang the
soprano. But there was a mistake in the manuscript in young
Burney's part, so that the duet went wrong and the master's
wrath was terrible indeed, until he realised that Smith the
copyist was at fault. Then he made an honourable apology to
the trembling young musician : ' I beg your barton – I am a
very odd tog – Maishter Schmidt is to blame.'

Mrs. Storer was a singer of quite another type, essentially
' English ' in her style. She first appeared on the Dublin stage
in 1743, but in December, 1742, she had sung with Dr. Arne's
wife in *Acis and Galatea*. In 1747 she sang Polly in *The Beggar's
Opera* at Covent Garden, and in 1749 she was at Dublin again
under Sheridan (Richard Brinsley Sheridan's father) for two

seasons with her husband, the Macklins, and the Lampes. The company went to Edinburgh in the winter of 1750-51, preceding the Ranelagh season, where, among other singing parts, she was Polly to Mrs. Lampe's Lucy, with her husband as Peachum. She also appeared as Ophelia, a part usually given to a singing actress in those days, when the Mad Scene was sometimes ' improved ' by the insertion of Purcell's Mad Bess.

One of the Ranelagh composers this season was James Oswald. Oswald was a Dunfermline dancing-master, who from 1736 onwards had some reputation in Edinburgh as violinist, dancing teacher and organist. In 1741 he came south and apparently enjoyed the patronage of his countryman, Lord Bute, the favourite of the Princess of Wales. It is possible he gave early music lessons to her son, the future George III, who was later to be a staunch supporter of music. Together with Burney, John Reid, afterwards General Reid, who founded the Reid Chair of Music at Edinburgh, and some others, he joined in a group which called itself ' The Society of the Temple of Apollo ' and published ' sundry airs, ballads, cantatas, and other light musical productions.' Their activities and ' Oswald's methods of publication remain still an open field for antiquarian detectives,' according to Dr. Percy Scholes[1]. Oswald's music shop was on the north side of St. Martin's Church, at the corner of St. Martin's Lane, and from that address he published music by himself and other composers, as well as that by the mysterious ' Society of the Temple of Apollo.' He was a popular composer of the Pleasure Gardens type of song.

* * *

In the 1752 season Abram Brown (or Abraham Browne)

[1] Proceedings of the Musical Association: A New Enquiry into the Life and Work of Dr. Burney, 1940-41.

THE
Perspective View
as intended to be finish'd
of the
Amphitheatrical Building
with part of the Garden
in which it is Erected at
Chelsea
Designd by Will. Jones

W. Jones fect et Del.

Explanation
A. The Amphitheatre 185 feet Diam.
B. Ranelagh House —— —— ——
C. The Great Barr —— —— ——
DD. Boxes for Gentlemen to Sweak in
E. Part of ye Great Walk leading to ye Thames
F. Part of the Canal —— —— ——
G. The New Bason —— —— ——
H. The Lady's Walk —— —— ——

AD June 21 1742 according to Act of Parliament

F.M. La Cave Sculp.

OTUNDA AND GARDENS

succeeded Michael Festing as leader of the orchestra. Festing's health and popularity had begun to decline in 1750, the rapid rise to fame of Giardini being one of the chief causes of this decline. Of Giardini something will be said later. Abram Brown was not in the same category as virtuoso or as musician ; Burney says he had ' a clear, sprightly and loud tone, with a strong hand,' but his music consisted of ' des notes, rien que des notes,' with no real musical knowledge or feeling behind them. He too played in the King's Band of Musick, and the Swan Tavern Concerts. Guilia Frasi and John Beard sang at concerts which began at twelve o'clock with ' breakfasting as usual,' until an Act of Parliament prohibited any place of entertainment from opening before a certain hour in the afternoon, and concerts were moved to the evenings. Amateur singers, impressed by Mr. Beard's singing of ' Fair Hebe ' or ' The Virgin's Last Resolve ' or ' Tom loves Mary passing well,' would find the words and sometimes the tune, with figured bass, in the musical supplements to the *London Magazine*, *The Universal Magazine* or *The Gentleman's Magazine*.

Ranelagh offered some non-musical and unrehearsed entertainment that summer. On May 6th there was an affray in the Rotunda, where conduct was usually so sedate, and Dr. John Hill – later Sir John Hill, first superintendent of the Royal Gardens at Kew – was caned. Then there were the two Miss Gunnings, forerunners of the Edwardian professional beauties, round whom crowds gathered when they were seen at Ranelagh or any other public place. They were the daughters of John Gunning of Castle Coote, Co. Roscommon, and so poor when they were presented to the Lord-Lieutenant of Ireland that the legend tells they had to borrow clothes for the occasion from Peg Woffington the actress. But when they came to London – Maria in her eighteenth year, and Elizabeth a year younger – their faces proved their fortunes. Maria had married George, sixth Earl of Coventry in March, and Elizabeth the Duke of Hamilton in February. Ten years later Maria died of consumption, brought on (so it was rumoured) by her use of white lead as a cosmetic, but Elizabeth lived for many years, became Duchess of Argyll some time after the death of her husband, and was as good as she was beautiful. That summer they were the sensation of London society.

In 1751 the calendar in this country was reformed to bring it into line with the New Style introduced in the Catholic countries by Gregory XIII in the sixteenth century. The year was to begin on 1st January, instead of as heretofore on 25th March, and eleven days were to be dropped out between September 2nd and 14th, 1752, so that the day after September 2nd should be called September 14th. The old-fashioned objected to this innovation, much as in recent years they objected to altering their clocks when summer time was introduced ; such a change was contrary to the will of God, and going against nature.

*　　*　　*

The years between the Peace of Aix-la-Chapelle and the outbreak of the Seven Years War gave England breathing space. Political life was relatively dull, and events abroad did not seem so important at the time as they were to prove in the future. Henry Pelham was Prime Minister, and at his death in 1754 was succeeded by his elder brother, the Duke of Newcastle. William Pitt was already powerful in Parliament, and a bitter opponent of Newcastle. It was a seed-time which was destined to produce a bumper crop of problems in due course.

Interest in those colonies was growing ever more keen among the promenaders in the Rotunda, however, and mistrust of France had another field in which to exercise itself. In India, the French were trying to build up an empire in the south, and would have succeeded in driving the East India Company out altogether if it had not been for Colonel Clive, and in Canada they were taking liberties with some of our forts, and driving the English traders out of the Ohio valley. But these disputes had not spread to European soil, and they were a long way off, after all.

' News there is none to tell you,' Walpole wrote in 1753, adding that he knew of nothing but elopements. Of news of that kind the patrons of Ranelagh always had plenty to discuss. There was also a Marriage Bill, which was intended to put a stop to elopements, or at least to clandestine marriages, such as that of Elizabeth Chudleigh. This entailed the proclaiming of banns, which Walpole thought ' an impudent ceremony.' There were, too, the perennial topics of masquerades, balls, executions and robberies. There was Handel's music, and the Italian opera, and Garrick at Drury Lane, and Fielding's novels, and Richardson's *Sir Charles Grandison*. Walpole's miniature Gothic castle at Strawberry Hill, Twickenham, was an important subject of conversation and correspondence during those years, and in 1754 one Thomas Chippendale, a cabinet-maker of St. Martin's Lane, published a *Gentleman's and Cabinet-maker's Directory*, to which joiners, carpenters and cabinet-makers subscribed as well as the nobility and gentry, in order to learn ' the pure Chinese manner ' or the Gothic, or a combination of the two, which was not so very unlike the Chinese-Venetian structure in the middle of Ranelagh's canal.

Smallpox was a threat to life and to beauty which was never far from people's thoughts, and in the early 50's the benefits of inoculation were much discussed. A poem on the subject appeared in the *Gentleman's Magazine* addressed to the smallpox, and 'inscribed to Miss N.B.,' a lady who had evidently decided to be inoculated. The following are some of the lines:–

> *Spoiler of beauty ! for this once forbear*
> *To print thy vengeance on this blooming fair*
>
> . . . . .
>
> *Wisely determined to prevent the foe*
> *Nor wait unguarded to sustain the blow,*
> *Bravely resolv'd the doubtful war to wage,*
> *She mocks thy fury and eludes thy rage.*

The first smallpox hospital was opened in 1746.

Interest in the British settlements in North America was growing. Readers of the *Gentleman's Magazine* could learn (among other curious facts) that the inhabitants of New York – one of the most flourishing of these settlements – had the reputation of being industrious and active. Now that the voyage from New York to Bristol occupied only four months, such information might be useful.

1754 was a particularly bad year for Ranelagh's music, for the Proprietors were refused a music licence. They did their best with public breakfastings, and there was an entertainment, consisting largely of recitations, under the name of *Comus's Court*. The Act for ' regulating places of public entertainment and punishing persons keeping disorderly houses ' which took effect on December 1st, 1752 bore hardly on the Pleasure Gardens. Ranelagh could scarcely be described as ' a disorderly house,' and in November of 1754 recovered its licence and continued its interrupted musical career. On December 26th peace was signed at Pondicherry between the English and French, who pledged themselves to non-intervention in the affairs of the Native Princes.

In 1755, John Stanley, the blind organist (1713 – 1786), was playing, and John Beard and one of the Misses Young were singing a Pastoral of Arne, with words by Shakespeare. (More will be said later about the Young-Arne family.)

III

1756–1763

THE SEVEN YEARS WAR

But when Ranelagh opened for breakfasts in February, 1756, the French King was ordering British subjects to leave Dunkirk, and seizing English vessels in his ports, and by the time the summer evening concerts were in full swing, the Seven Years War had begun. The Duke of Newcastle was driven from office, and William Pitt was Prime Minister. Many a gallant sailor now defending our shores against the French must have thought nostalgically not only of his home, but of the amusements of Ranelagh and of 'the Fair' with whom he had strolled in the Gardens or promenaded in the Rotunda. The anonymous N — sent to the *Gentleman's Magazine* that year a 'Song from on board the Fleet; inscribed to the Ladies,' in which he says :—

> *Ye muses, who carol the nymphs and the swains*
> *Who love to be sporting in gardens and plains,*
> *Leave Marybon's frolics and Ranelagh's glee,*
> *And give us a moment your presence at sea.*

Tho' banish'd the midnight assemblies and shows,
Good humour of ladies, and folly of beaux ;
'Tis truth I aver, howe'er strange it may read,
We're ne'er from your elbow though here at Spithead.

. . . . . .

Thus pleasure imagin'd is pleasure refin'd,
Tho' absent in person, we're present in mind ;
Round each giddy circle your steps we pursue,
And act the scenes o'er again, ladies, with you.

Many letter-writers must have agreed with Walpole that though war was a dreadful calamity, yet it was ' a very comfortable commodity for writing letters,' especially after such dull years. As usual, things went badly in the beginning. Minorca fell into the hands of the French almost immediately following Admiral Byng's indecisive engagement with Admiral Galissonière, which resulted in the British Admiral being court-martialled and shot the following March, ' pour encourager les autres ' as Voltaire said. News came slowly, and the patrons of Ranelagh did not know for a long time that while they were circling round the amphitheatre on June 18th, 1757, listening to music or scandal, or enjoying cool breezes from the river in the Gardens, Calcutta had been attacked by Suraja Dowla, and that 123 of their countrymen were being suffocated to death in a dungeon that was later to be known as the Black Hole. Handel's *Acis and Galatea* was given at Ranelagh that summer for the benefit of the Marine Society, which had just been started by subscription, mainly among the gentlemen at White's, at the instigation of Justices Fielding and Welch ; upwards of 260 vagrant and friendless boys were clothed and sent on board the Fleet. On June 2nd the Foundling Hospital was opened, for the reception of unwanted children under two months old. The

age may have been one of scepticism, brutality and frivolity,
but practical piety and social conscience became more and
more apparent as the century wore on.

Ranelagh's architect, William Jones, died on November
19th, 1757, and was compared with Inigo Jones by one
panegyrist :—

> *If nature's taste by judgement's rules refin'd*
> *And apt invention, grace an artist's mind,*
> *If such an artist's loss demands your moans,*
> Britons *lament, you've lost a second* Jones.

*   *   *

In the summer of 1758, when Colonel Clive was winning
the battle of Plassey, and Mr. Pitt had just become premier
at the head of a new ministry, Kitty Fourmantel (or Catherine
de Fourmantelles) – Laurence Sterne's ' dear, dear Jenny,'
his ' sweet lass ' – was singing at Ranelagh, though it was not
for another year that he met her. Oswald was still composing
for Ranelagh, and Miss Fourmantel sang his songs. She came
of a French Protestant family that had left France at the
Revocation of the Edict of Nantes, and was said to have been
governess for a time, before she became a professional singer,
to the children of the Countess of Bristol. But more of her later.

1759 was the year of victories, ' the wonderful year,' but
it produced no victory music to compare with the Dettingen
Te Deum or *Judas Maccabæus*, for blind Mr. Handel had died
in April. But there was a crop of topical songs at Ranelagh and
all the places of entertainment in the country, most of which
have been deservedly forgotten. ' Heart of Oak,' the air which
Dr. Boyce wrote for the bass Champness to sing in Garrick's
Harlequin's Invasion, however, has long outlived the occasion
for which it was written.

Yet though the war was obviously going well in the more

distant parts of the globe, the menace of invasion from our nearest neighbour was never far from the minds of the promenaders that season. In June the Rotunda was emptied of ' all the smart gentlemen,' for they were gone with the Militia. Knights of shires who had never shot anything but woodcock presented a fine martial appearance when the King reviewed them in Hyde Park. In July the French had been actually seen disembarking at Deal by an officer who rode post-haste to London with the news, but it proved to be another rumour. Three weeks later there were bonfires and squibs to celebrate the battle of Minden, and in September the country rejoiced in the victory of Quebec, and mourned the death of General Wolfe.

Dr. Percy Scholes, in his Musical Association Paper[1] has proved that it was this very year at Ranelagh that Mr. Burney's burlesque musical setting of Bonnell Thornton's *Ode to St. Cecilia* was first performed. It was ' adapted to the ancient British music, *viz.* the salt-box and jews-harp, the marrow-bones and cleaver, the hum-strum or hurdy-gurdy.' John Beard sang the Salt-Box Song, accompanied on that unusual instrument by Mr. Brent, a well-known fencing master and father of the singer, Charlotte Brent, who will shortly appear in these pages. The music has been lost, and the following specimen of the words will probably suffice :–

> *In strains more exalted the salt-box shall join,*
> *And clattering and battering and clapping combine*
> *With a rap and a tap while the hollow side sounds,*
> *Up and down leaps the flap, and with rattling resounds.*

* * *

Kitty Fourmantel was singing at the York Subscription Concerts at the Assembly Rooms that winter, and among

[1] *op. cit.*

other occasions she sang on November 29th, the day of general rejoicings for Lord Hawke's victory. It was then that Laurence Sterne first met her, and there began that curious *amitié amoureuse* between them, a strange compound of playful philandering, sincere friendship and that ' sentiment ' which was almost Sterne's invention and which was to be a new element in eighteenth-century relations between men and women, both in literature and life. He sent her pots of sweetmeats and honey, with tender messages, and also sermons ; he called her ' sweet lass ' and his ' dear, dear Jenny,' assured her of the truest friendship ever man bore woman, and told her he would give a guinea for a squeeze of her hand. Yet there is no evidence she was his mistress. Truly a strange state of affairs for the eighteenth century. But Sterne was a strange being. She, on her side, spoke of him as a kind and generous friend whom Providence had sent to her in York where she was a stranger.

In March, Sterne was in London, enjoying the fame which had come to him from the publication of the first volume of *Tristram Shandy*, and in April there was some disappointment about Kitty's Ranelagh engagement. But soon she was settled with her mother at Meard's Court, Soho, and singing at Ranelagh with Beard and Miss Stevenson. Among their repertoire that season were songs by Joseph Baildon, one of the tribe of Pleasure Gardens composers, who was born in 1727 and died in 1774. Two years after these Ranelagh songs (published in September of 1760) he contributed some of the music to *Love in a Village*, one of the most successful and charming of the English light operas (miscalled ballad operas) which did as much as the Pleasure Gardens songs to keep native singing fresh and alive. He was also a popular composer of glees, a form of music to which the eighteenth century was much addicted, and of which we shall hear something in connection with Ranelagh later. Did Sterne himself write the words of a song in praise of Jenny, which John Beard must have sung ?

> *Tho' Diamonds shine brighter than Jenny's bright Eyes,*
> *And her cheeks are outblush'd by the Rose,*
> *Tho' no Flow'rets around her sweet Steps deign to rise*
> *And her Skin is not whiter than Snows ;*
>
> . . . . . .
>
> *Yet her Charms are as great as a Woman can boast,*
> *And her Virtues are equall'd by few ;*
> *She's too good for a Belle, she's too wise for a Toast ;*
> *And I love her—ay, that's what I do !*

While Sterne was being lionised and writing ' sentimental ' letters that spring to his Kitty, and she was planning to come up to London with her mother, Lord Ferrers was being tried at Westminster Hall for the murder of his steward. He was subsequently hanged at Tyburn. It was one of the most impressive executions of the century, which no amateur of such spectacles would have missed. Instead of riding in a mourning coach, Lord Ferrers went to the gallows in his own landau drawn by six horses, and wore his wedding suit. By mistake, he presented a gratuity of five guineas to the executioner's assistant instead of to the executioner himself ; this occasioned an unseemly wrangle, which the condemned man had to settle himself before meeting his end with a fortitude which moved all the spectators. The previous year Elizabeth Chudleigh, ' Iphigenia,' had taken the first step on a very devious road which was to carry her in another sixteen years to Westminster Hall, though not to Tyburn. Augustus Hervey's elder brother, the Earl of Bristol, was in failing health, and she saw some prospect of being a countess if she could establish her secret marriage ; she therefore had it entered on the Church register, where it could be referred to if necessary. Meanwhile, it was still a secret, and she was the mistress of the Duke of Kingston.

About the same time Lord George Sackville was court-martialled for having disobeyed his superior officer, Prince Ferdinand of Brunswick, at the battle of Minden, and neglected to advance with his cavalry. He was ' adjudged unfit to serve his Majesty in any military capacity whatever,' and his name removed from the list of privy councillors, but he was spared the fate of Admiral Byng.

Truly, the Rotunda had plenty to talk about that summer.

*   *   *

William Whitehead, the Poet Laureate, wrote an Ode for the New Year of 1761, which was set to music by Dr. Boyce, and performed before the King, in which he asked the universe :—

> *Still must the muse, indignant, hear,*
> *The clanging trump, the rattling car,*
> *And usher in each opening year*
> *With groans of death and sounds of war ?*

The indignant muse was to hear a good deal more noise in the course of that year. Indeed, 1761 might be called the year of salvos and fireworks ; what with victories, a royal wedding and a coronation, the guns in the Park had scarce time to cool, Horace Walpole said, and we were nearly ruining ourselves in gunpowder and skyrockets. George II had died suddenly the previous October, and when Ranelagh opened for the season of 1761, everyone was still rejoicing in the accession of a young King, British-born, of Protestant piety, simple tastes and unblemished morals, who told Parliament he ' gloried in the name of Briton,' and who could scarcely find the Electorate of Hanover on the map. At his levee he walked about, and spoke to everyone, instead of standing on one spot with his eyes fixed royally on the ground, ' dropping bits of German news.' It was a drawback certainly, that he had been for so long under the thumb of his mother and of her unpopular Scots favourite, Lord Bute, but now that he was King it was hoped he would shake off these undesirable influences. The new reign opened very promisingly. His narrow-mindedness, mental instability and obstinacy were blemishes which only gradually became apparent in George III ; his many virtues were of just the kind to make an immediate appeal to the British public. There were other causes of satisfaction : the war was going well, and there were hopes of peace, for in July Mr. Stanley was in Paris and the Abbé de Bussy in London, negotiating.

Laurence Sterne sauntered in Ranelagh Gardens with Mrs. Vesey, the fair blue-stocking. Never until he saw her did he imagine that grace could be so perfect in all its parts. Poor Kitty was put in the shade, it seems, but perhaps they listened to her singing in the Rotunda, and Sterne gave her flowers or pressed her hand after the performance.

Farther up the river, a very large piece of *chinoiserie* was becoming visible : Sir William Chambers' pagoda in Kew Gardens was growing so fast that in July it could be seen from Twickenham.

The peace negotiations fell through, but the King's marriage to Princess Charlotte of Mecklenburg-Strelitz and the coronation of their Majesties in September were sufficient causes of rejoicing. At the coronation, Ranelagh's Sir Thomas Robinson represented the Duke of Normandy, walking next the Archbishop of Canterbury. This was the last time the Dukes of Normandy and Aquitaine were represented as doing homage at a coronation of a British King.

Dr. Arne composed a serenata for Ranelagh called *Beauty and Virtue* in honour of the royal nuptials, which was sung by Mr. Tenducci, Miss Brent, Mr. Champness and Master

Johnson. Songs from Dr. Arne's new opera *Artaxerxes* were also included in the programme.

The next few years were to be Ranelagh's most interesting period musically, a period dominated by Dr. Arne, whose music is so full of sweetness and whose character was so full of asperities. He did not write all the music for Ranelagh during the 60's, nor can he have superintended it always, for he was a man of many activities. But for many years his music predominated, and the Ranelagh singers were nearly all connected with him in some way ; they were his wife's relations, or his pupils, or had sung in his operas. This, therefore, seems the place in which to speak of the Arne-Young clan.

It is in the days of Handel's later operas and early oratorios that we first come across the exceedingly talented and exceedingly confusing Young family. (' The race of Youngs are *born* songsters and musicians,' said Mrs. Delany.) Hawkins and Burney both made pardonable errors in the family tree, and even now one or two points remain to be cleared up. Dr. Charles Young, organist of All Hallows, Barking, son of Dr. Anthony Young, organist of St. Clement Danes and St. Catherine Cree, had three, possibly four, daughters and one son. All three daughters, possibly four, were well-known singers from roughly 1732-1759. Cecilia, the most famous, married Dr. Arne in 1737 ; Isabella married the composer Lampe, shortly after 1737 ; a more shadowy ' Miss Young ' became Mrs. Jones at some date not yet discovered – her Christian name is sometimes given as Mary, and sometimes as Esther, and it is this which has suggested to the present writer the possibility that Mary and Esther were two different people, both singers. But three are confusing enough, and of the three, Mrs. Arne and Mrs. Lampe alone need concern us. To add to our difficulties, their brother Charles, who was in the Treasury, had two daughters who were as celebrated in their generation as their aunts had been in theirs; one was Isabella, and the other Polly or Mary, and they both sang as ' Miss Young ' until their respective marriages to the Hon. John Scott and Francis Barthelemon. As if this were not enough, Dr. Arne's son, Michael, was twice married and each time to a professional singer, so that towards the end of the century we have two more Mrs. Arnes. Mrs. Lampe also had a singer daughter-in-law singing as Mrs. Lampe.

Of the three (or possibly four) Miss Youngs of the first generation, Cecilia is the one whose singing and personality most impressed her contemporaries. She was born in 1711, and studied with Geminiani, the violinist and author of *A Treatise of Good Taste in the Art of Music* (1742), which deals both with playing and singing. Although he was an instrumentalist himself and evidently taught the pure *bel canto* singing, which aimed at making the voice as flexible and obedient as any instrument, Geminiani regarded technique as only the means to an end. He complains of those players and singers who think of nothing but making ' continually some favourite Passages or Graces,' and he once told a well-known singer : ' Your Execution is exceedingly great, but you have not in the least affected me ; my *ears* were entertained, but my *heart* was at rest.' Cecilia acquired from him the ' Italian style,' but she could sing in her own language as well. It is possible that the Young family inherited traditions going back to Purcell's time, since Dr. Anthony Young, Cecilia's grandfather, left the Chapel Royal when his voice broke in 1700, and it is very likely he was the son of William Young, violinist in the King's Band. If this is so, then the Youngs inherited the best traditions of both the Italian and the English schools of singing. Cecilia must have been coached by Handel, since she sang in *Ariodante* and *Alcina* in 1735, and *Alexander's Feast* in 1736. She probably studied with Dr. Arne, whom she married in 1737, but it seems also likely that she

passed on to him some of the *bel canto* traditions she had received from Geminiani, for there is no doubt that Dr. Arne
taught 'the florid style,' although his English ballads helped
to keep alive the English style. Cecilia had indeed every qualification a singer needs, except one – good health. Burney says
there was a time ' when her voice, shape and manner of singing
were superior to those of any other female singer in this country,' and gratefully acknowledges that he learnt much ' from
accompanying her in her vocal exercises.' Cecilia was evidently
a musician as well as a singer. She was a kind woman, too, and
not only assisted young Burney's ' professional improvement,'
but had a ' parental interest ' in his morals and conduct. Her
greatest period seems to have been from 1735–1745; from
1742–1744 she was in Dublin with her husband, singing in his
Comus, Rosamund, Judgment of Paris, Alfred and in various
interludes and concerts. It was the high-tide of both their
careers, and whatever their domestic relations, their musical
partnership was certainly harmonious. Yet even then she was
constantly battling with ill-health. The partnership was continued when they returned to London in 1745, and Cecilia
sang frequently at Drury Lane and Vauxhall, though not (as
far as I have been able to discover) at Ranelagh. In 1755 they
were back in Dublin for the first performance of Dr. Arne's
Eliza, which had to be postponed because of Cecilia's illness.
With them was Charlotte Brent, Dr. Arne's brilliant pupil,
for whom his more showy music was written, and who will be
further mentioned presently. After the Dublin season Dr.
Arne left his wife, and they were not reconciled for twenty
years. She remained behind in Dublin in poor health and
poorer circumstances, but with her young niece Polly Young,
who was later to appear at Ranelagh as Mrs. Barthelemon. Mrs.
Delany said she had been ' severely used by a bad husband,
and suffered to starve, if she had not met with charitable
people.' Bad health had interrupted her career – in fact, she

made only a few more appearances in public – and she supported herself by teaching. Aunt and niece came back to London some time between 1759-1762, and in 1770 she was obliged to appeal to her husband through a lawyer, saying that even the small sum he allowed her, ' which fell greatly short of supplying her with common necessities,' was in arrear. The correspondence which ensued shows the successful Dr. Arne in his least amiable light, while his neglected and unfortunate wife lost neither her dignity nor her charity. Fanny Burney says of Dr. Arne that he ' scoffed at all other but musical reputation,' and his correspondence with Garrick and others is sufficient to show that he was quarrelsome and touchy. But before he died he was reconciled to his wife, and for the last few months of his life they seem to have lived happily together.

There is no evidence that Cecilia sang at Ranelagh during what I have called the reign of Dr. Arne. In the 60's she was separated from her husband, and had practically given up singing through ill-health, although she made one appearance on the London Stage as Mandane in *Artaxerxes* in 1769. But she was one of the most important of the Young–Arne clan of singers, and her influence on those of the next generation, particularly on Mary Young II (or Polly), later Mrs. Barthelemon, is enough of itself to give her a place in this chapter.

Her sister, Isabella Young I, was also well known as singer and actress, and has already been mentioned once or twice in the course of this narrative. She married the composer Lampe soon after the first performance of his *Dragon of Wantley*, and sang both at the London Pleasure Gardens and theatres, as well as in the provinces. She was with Mrs. Arne in Dublin in 1748.

In 1755 ' Miss Young ' was in Dublin with Mrs. Arne and their niece Mary Young II (or Polly). Was this Esther or Mary, or Mary-Esther? It has not much consequence, perhaps.

and musicians,' Mrs. Delany truly said, and Polly seems (like her aunt) to have been musician as well as singer, for at nine years old she accompanied 'most surprisingly' on the harpsichord. It seems she was apprenticed to the Arnes, after the eighteenth-century fashion, and this apprenticeship was a further source of dispute between the Doctor and his wife after their separation.

Polly made her début at Drury Lane on September 30th, 1762, singing and playing the harpsichord. She was introduced by John Beard himself, which 'with the agreeable innocence of her appearance (for she is scarce in her teens) greatly pre-possessed the audience in her favour . . . those who were judges, pronounced that she would one day reach the summit of musical perfection. Her performance on the harpsichord is equal to her excellent singing.' In 1763 she was engaged for the King's Theatre in the Haymarket, afterwards singing alternately at the King's Theatre and Covent Garden. When her sister Isabella had a benefit at Ranelagh in 1766, tickets were obtainable from Miss Young 'next door to the Wheatsheaf.' This was possibly Polly, and it seems likely that aunt and nieces were living together. In 1766 she was a member of the 'serious' as opposed to the 'burletta' company at the King's Theatre, and in the course of that year she married Francis Barthelemon. François Hippolyte Barthelemon had been born at Bordeaux in 1741. As violinist and composer he was well known in London during the last thirty years of the century, and in 1776 he and his wife undertook a tour in Europe. In Florence his *Jepthah* was performed with success, with his wife and Signor Roncaglia as the chief soloists. It was repeated in Rome, and a chorus from it was sung by the Sistine Choir. At Naples they performed at the Queen's private concerts, and when they returned to London *via* Paris they carried with them a letter in the Queen of Naples's own writing to her sister, Queen Marie Antoinette of France. Marie Antoinette gave a ' select party at her chateau at Versailles,' and ' desired the Barthelemons to attend,' on which occasion Polly's singing of a bravura air from *Jepthah* with violin obbligato by her husband was 'especially admired' by Her Majesty. They returned to England in 1777, and both performed regularly at the chief Pleasure Gardens, as will be seen later. The pair became interested in the doctrines of Swedenborg, as preached by the Rev. Jacob Duché, and at some point in his connection with the New Church, Barthelemon composed the music to Ken's hymn ' Awake my Soul,' and other music for the Asylum for Female Orphans in St. George's Fields. Mrs. Barthelemon's compositions included ' The Weaver's Prayer,' sung by her at a concert in aid of ' Distress'd Weavers,' and an ' Ode on the late Providential Preservation of our Most Gracious Sovereign.' When Mrs. Arne came to live with the Barthelemons, after Dr. Arne's death, the religious atmosphere of the home must have been curious, for Mrs. Arne was a strict and very pious Catholic. But when she was dying in 1789, notwithstanding the difference in their forms of religious belief, they all read the psalms and lessons together beside her bed over which hung a crucifix. Barthelemon himself seems to have suffered from something like religious mania, and when Haydn came to see him in the 90's, he found him ' very devout and gloomy.' A gloomy religion must have been difficult for Haydn to understand. Mrs. Barthelemon died in 1799, her husband not till 1808, but the Young tradition was carried on well into the nineteenth century, by their child, Cecilia, named after her great-aunt. She made a début as a singer when she was about eleven years old, and later composed both for piano and harpsichord, but on her marriage to Captain Henslowe she seems to have given up music. It was little Cecilia who brought Dr. Arne and his wife together after their long estrangement, and one of her earliest recollections was of kneeling beside her great-aunt Arne at the

K

foot of Dr. Arne's bed, and hearing him sing a short Alleluia as he was dying.

So much for Dr. Arne's wife's relations, who will appear from time to time in Ranelagh's story. His only direct descendant seems to have been Michael, born in 1740, an illegitimate son, according to Burney. He too was a singer, though not a very successful one, and his compositions have been overshadowed by his father's, his best-known song, ' The Lass with a Delicate Air,' being all too often attributed to Dr. Arne. He wrote many songs for the theatre and the Pleasure Gardens, especially for Ranelagh. In character, he seems to have been as unstable as his father ; he was constantly in debt, and spent much of his time and money trying to find the Philosopher's Stone. His first wife was Elizabeth Wright, a very sweet singer and excellent actress at Drury Lane and the Pleasure Gardens, whom he is said to have ' sung to death.' She died some time before 1775 (in 1769 she is described as ' very ill at Bristol '). After her death he married again, another singer, who seems to have survived him. He wore out not only his first wife, but their daughter also ; her health was so impaired by her nursing of him in his last illness that she had to give up her own promising singing career for a while, and confine herself to instrumental teaching. Later, however, she recovered her voice, and had some success as a singer at the end of the eighteenth and beginning of the nineteenth century.

Thus there were three Mrs. Arnes and one Miss Arne singing at different times during the century, as well as Dr. Arne's sister, Mrs. Cibber, who sang as Miss Arne in her early days, and two Master Arnes – Dr. Arne's brother, Michael, who sang in the first performance of *Rosamund*, and his son Michael. And there were at least five, possibly six, Miss Youngs who were singers, as well as a distinguished actress of the same name.

Here we can leave the Arne–Young clan, but this seems a suitable place in which to say something of Dr. Arne's most famous pupil, who has already been mentioned in connection with the Dublin visits – Charlotte Brent. She was the daughter of a singer who sang in Handel's oratorios, and of Brent the fencing-master. She had a high and very flexible soprano voice which Dr. Arne trained ' in the Italian style,' and for which he wrote the florid part of Mandane in *Artaxerxes*. He brought her out in *Eliza* in Dublin in 1755, as already stated, and three years later she sang the same part at Drury Lane. Garrick was not impressed by her voice, and refused to give her a permanent engagement, telling Dr. Arne that not all his vocal geese were swans. In any case, music at Drury Lane was at best ' pickle to my roast beef,' to which Dr. Arne replied, ' Then, by God, Davy, your beef shall be well pickled before I have done.' He carried out his threat, by taking his pupil to the rival house, Covent Garden, where John Beard engaged her. Beard played Macheath to her Polly, and Garrick's audience streamed to Covent Garden, until he found a rival Polly and a rival Macheath in Mrs. Vincent and Thomas Lowe. But Charlotte Brent was now well established. Her brilliant, showy style of singing undoubtedly had a great influence on Dr. Arne's style of vocal writing ; particularly in the part of Mandane, which she first performed in February, 1762, he crowded all ' the Italian divisions and difficulties which had ever been heard of in opera,' as Burney put it. The essentially English charm of his early Pleasure Gardens songs, his *Comus*, his *Alfred* and the Shakespeare songs was gone. In 1766 Charlotte Brent married Thomas Pinto, the violinist, and continued to sing for many years under the name of Mrs. Pinto. After his death, and when she could no longer sing, she lived in great poverty, and died on April 10th, 1802.

*   *   *

In the summer of 1762, just after the first performance of *Artaxerxes*, Miss Brent was singing at Ranelagh, and doubtless she favoured the audience with ' The Soldier tir'd of War's Alarms,' which was to an eighteenth-century florid soprano what *Caro Nome* or the Mad Song from *Lucia* are to her twentieth-century equivalent. With her was Miss Thomas – a young singer who afterwards made a good name for herself in oratorio. More important were Champness and Tenducci.

Champness has already been mentioned as the first singer of ' Heart of Oak ' in *Harlequin's Invasion*. He was an outstanding bass and had sung in the Foundling Hospital *Messiah* under J. C. Smith in the same ' wonderful year,' with Mrs. Scott, and was a regular Drury Lane singer. He and John Beard appeared as the singing witches in Garrick's version of *Macbeth*, wearing ' mittens, plaited caps, laced aprons, red stomachers, ruffs, etc.' (' Beggarly gammers,' Oulton called them.)

When we read of the great *natural* voices of the past, we can at least imagine what they sounded like by analogy with some of the great voices of the present. Almost unconsciously, we imagine Cecilia Arne to have sung like, say, Elizabeth Schumann or Isobel Baillie, Charlotte Brent like Galli Curci, John Beard like Walter Widdop, Champness like Norman Walker or William Parsons, according to our individual taste in singers. But there is nothing in our musical experience that can give us any idea of the singing of Ferdinando Tenducci. The castrato voice is heard no more, and there is no one living who can tell us what it sounded like. We shall never hear *Care Selve* or *Ombra mai fù*, for instance, sung by the type of voice for which they were written. We can only take on trust from contemporary accounts that the greatest voices of this kind – Senesino, Farinelli, Cafarelli, Marchesi, Pacchierotti – were of extraordinary beauty and manipulated with the highest degree of *bel canto* technique. By the 60's, as has been seen, the tenor voice was already taking a leading part in vocal music, and the days of the male soprano or contralto were numbered, though that may not have been realised. Ferdinando Tenducci was not as great a singer as the five mentioned above, but he was much admired in his day, and played a considerable part in the musical life of London, Dublin and Edinburgh. He had been born in Siena in about

M.ʳ Linly

SIX

New English Songs

Composed by

FERDINANDO TENDUCCI

and to be Sung by him at Ranelagh

Price 5.ˢ

Printed for the Author.
And to be had of him at his Lodgings in the Great Piazza Covent-Garden, the Corner of James Street;
and at all the Musick Shops.
Where may be had the Instrumental parts altogether.—Price 10.ˢ 6.ᵈ
N3. The Horns, Flutes, Hautboys, and Bassoons are particularly Obligated.

1763

1736, and came to London in 1758 to sing in the Italian opera. He sang Arbaces in the first performance of Dr. Arne's *Artaxerxes*, with Miss Brent, and John Beard. One of his greatest achievements was his singing of 'Water parted from the Sea' from that opera; O'Keefe says it created a furore when it was first heard in Dublin, and in Domenico Corri's *Select Airs* we can see written out all the ornaments which he introduced into it, probably with the composer's approval. In 1765 he went to Dublin for three years, and while there, somewhat surprisingly, eloped with a pupil, and married her.

Less surprisingly, the marriage was annulled in 1775. He reappeared in London later in the century, but his Ranelagh period seems to have been his finest. (He was then in his twenties.) Like nearly all great *bel canto* singers, he was an all-round musician, and composed a number of pleasant songs, as well as a treatise on singing.

When Miss Brent sang at Ranelagh in the summer of 1762 about the soldier being tired of war's alarms, many in her audience must have agreed with her. Our recent victories and conquests filled some minds with such pride and exultation that they forgot the cost at which they were bought, but others, like Walpole, were less empire-minded and sighed for peace. When he heard of the conquest of Martinique, his comment was : ' Well ! I wish we had conquered the world, and had done ! I think we were full as happy when we were a peaceable quiet set of tradesfolks, as now we are heir-apparent to the Romans, and overrunning the East and West Indies.' He admitted that he had ' no public spirit ' and did not ' care a farthing for the interests of the merchants.' If Guadeloupe or Martinique were given up, the price of sugar would fall, and the City would suffer. Horace Walpole, whose father's fortune had been founded on successful speculation at the time of the South Sea Bubble, had not much sympathy with the new class which was making fortunes out of the expanding empire. Nor could he approve any wealth which was derived from violence or bloodshed. ' Soldiers and sailors who are knocked on the head, and peasants plundered or butchered are to my eyes as valuable as a lazy, luxurious set of men who hire others to acquire riches for them. . . . I am a bad Englishman, because I think the advantages of commerce are dearly bought for some by the lives of many more.' He looked back nostalgically to his youth, when we were ' a peacable quiet set of tradesfolks ' and his father had kept the country out of all foreign entanglements.

IV

1763 – 1775

AGAIN BETWEEN TWO WARS

But the Seven Years War did come to an end at last in 1763, with the Peace of Paris, a peace which made us stronger than we were at any time in the course of the century. French fashions appeared in London once more. French milliners came to England, and the nobility and gentry visited Paris, bringing back with them the latest fantasy with which they enlivened the somewhat staid court. (Queen Charlotte avoided extremes of fashion, and was almost ' homely.') Ladies' hoops were larger than ever, oblong in shape and broader than they were high, but so contrived that each side could be raised to enable the wearer to sidle through doorways. Waists were narrow, the very low-cut bodices were sometimes draped with a lace fichu, and ruches encircled swan-like necks. (Ladies with short necks were well-advised to eschew this fashion.) Ladies' heads were still small, and powder was still worn. Feather muffs were one of the whims of the early sixties.

The commercial prosperity brought by such an advantage-ous peace naturally encouraged extravagance in dress. London merchants and 'nabobs' had made fortunes, which their wives were happy to help them spend. All sorts of luxuries were imported from the expanded Empire.

The reign of Dr. Arne at Ranelagh, in fact, coincided with the most prosperous period of the eighteenth century. Miss Brent and Tenducci were joined that summer by Miss Wright (later Mrs. Michael Arne, of whom something has already been said), and Mr. Dearle or D'Earl, whose voice seems to have been a tenor of somewhat limited range, judged by his repertoire.

*   *   *

By the season of 1764 there were already signs that the peace was being thrown away. The very strength of our new imperial position aroused fears and jealousies among the nations of Europe, and brought problems and responsibilities which could only have been shouldered by able statesmen. But Pitt was in retirement, exhausted by the war that he was largely responsible for winning, and we were to have ten years of government by a succession of short-sighted mediocrities, and of increasing interference by the King. Mr. Wilkes had attacked the King in No. 45 of the *North Briton* in April, 1763. Feeling was running high during the summer about Wilkes' expulsion from the House of Commons. Lord Bute was becoming more and more unpopular, and there were signs that those American Colonies might be going to make trouble. But the King and Queen gave an edifying example of family life to their subjects ; indeed, they lived so privately and frugally at Richmond during the summer months, that it was said that they were waited on by the Queen's hairdresser at dinner, and that only four pounds of beef were allowed for their soup.

Meanwhile, the best of modern music was to be heard at Ranelagh, very often with a ball and refreshments thrown in as good measure. At Miss Brent's benefit, Handel's *Samson* was performed, conducted by Dr. Arne; tickets were to be obtained from Miss Brent herself, next door to the China Shop in the Piazza near the Church, Covent Garden. ' Let the bright Seraphim ' must have been an aria after Miss Brent's heart. At Mr. Tenducci's ' night ' on June 18th, a good Choir of Singers was to be disposed over the orchestra, ' with some extraordinary hands,' which in modern English means ' augmented orchestra.' Besides ' the usual favourite songs ' (selections from Mr. Tenducci's repertoire) there were choruses from *Acis and Galatea* and *Alexander's Feast*, as well as ' The Lord God Omnipotent reigneth,' and the Coronation Anthem. In between the four parts of the concert, French horns and clarinets played Favourite Pieces in the Chinese Temple, while the ladies and gentlemen took the air in the Gardens. (Clarinets were still regarded chiefly as ' outdoor ' instruments and were not yet part of an indoor ' band of music,' although they were certainly heard in the overture to Dr. Arne's *Thomas and Sally* in 1760.) The whole concluded with a ball, and tickets for the entire entertainment, including tea and coffee, were only five shillings, obtainable at the Rainbow Coffee House, opposite the Royal Exchange, or from Mr. Tenducci himself, at his lodgings at Mr. Robinson's, King Street, Covent Garden. (It will be noticed that most of the Ranelagh artists lived around the Piazza.)

Among the instrumental soloists at this time was the 'cellist, Pasqualino. Caporale, Cervetto the elder and Pasqualino were pioneers in playing what was, after all, still a comparatively new instrument that was just superseding the viol da gamba. The two last had ' infinitely more hand, and knowledge of the finger-board, as well as of music generally,' Burney considered, but they had not Caporale's ' sweet and vocal tone.' For Pasqualino's Ranelagh benefit there was not only ' the usual vocal and instrumental concert,' but a ' grand Firework,' under the

MOZART, SIX YEARS OLD,
IN THE GALA SUIT PRESENTED TO HIM IN 1762 BY MARIA THERESA.
(*Engraved from a photograph of the original now in the Mozart Museum at Salzburg.*)

direction of Mr. Angelo, and performed by Mr. Benjamin Clitherow. No expense was spared to make this ' an elegant entertainment.'

Domenico Angelo Malevolti Tremando was a native of Leghorn, who established himself in this country as a master of equitation and fencing, and instructed the Royal Family as well as the nobility and gentry in those arts. He was one of the best-known men in London, and at his table Wilkes and Sheridan, as well as musicians, actors and foreign visitors, were to be met. Besides being a recognised authority on gentlemanly deportment – to which fencing and riding were essentials – he seems often to have been called in to arrange entertainments at Ranelagh and elsewhere, and undoubtedly had a good sense of *mise en scène*. His son, Henry Angelo, will be spoken of later.

A week after Pasqualino's benefit, the concert was ' For the benefit of a Public useful Charity,' which is surmised to have been the Lying-in Hospital (Surrey), of which the foundation stone was laid that year. The ' very favourite Chorus ' from *Acis and Galatea*, ' Oh the pleasures of the plains,' the song and chorus ' Oh happy pair ' from *Alexander's Feast* (in which Tenducci presumably sang the solo), and the Coronation Anthem were on the programme, as they had been when Tenducci took his own benefit. And ' in the Course of the Evening's Entertainments, the celebrated and astonishing Master MOZART, lately arrived, a Child of 7 years of Age, will perform several fine select Pieces of his own Composition on the Harpsichord and on the Organ, which has already given the highest Pleasure, Delight and Surprize to the greatest Judges of Music in England or Italy, and is justly esteemed the most extraordinary Prodigy, and most amazing Genius that has appeared in any Age.'

In point of fact the Child was then eight and a half, but in other respects the writer in the *Public Advertiser* spoke more truth than he probably realised. Leopold Mozart wrote to Lorenz Hagenauer at Salzburg on June 28th that he was ' letting Wolfgang play a concerto on the organ at this concert in order to perform thereby the act of an English patriot who, as far as in him lies, endeavours to further the usefulness of this hospital which has been established *pro bono publico.* That is, you see, one way of winning the affection of this quite exceptional nation.' Leopold counted on the presence in the Rotunda of that aristocracy he was so anxious to win over, with a view to earning more of those good English guineas.

Unfortunately, we have no account of the concert from Leopold, because in his next letter – dated over a month later – he is too full of the illness which he had contracted as the result of hurrying behind the sedan chair which carried his two children to Lord Thanet's concert in Grosvenor Square, and then sitting in a draught. (The windows were all open, English fashion.) When he was well enough, he was carried in a sedan chair to a house with a garden belonging to a Dr. Randal in Fivefields Row in the village of Chelsea (now Lower Ebury Street), where the air was supposed to be particularly favourable to convalescence. The family stayed there for seven weeks, and there Wolfgang wrote his symphonies K.16 and K.19, giving specially good parts to the horns, because he had been struck by the excellence of English horn players. He must have heard many river music parties passing up and down the Thames. It was late in the Ranelagh season when the Mozarts settled at Chelsea, and the children were so strictly kept that it is unlikely they were allowed to visit the Gardens while their father was ill. In all, the Mozarts were fifteen months in England. Soon after their arrival on April 23rd, they played before King George and Queen Charlotte. Master Wolfgang accompanied the young Queen in a song, and improvised both on the harpsichord and the organ ; indeed, his organ-playing was rated even higher than his clavier-playing.

*   *   *

By the summer, the golden age which the new reign and the Peace of Paris had seemed to usher in was already looking rather tarnished. Pitt, who had never enjoyed the King's confidence, had given up office, and in March, George Grenville, the Prime Minister, passed the American Stamp Act through Parliament. In April, George III had his first attack of insanity, and in May crowds of weavers marched about for four days, carrying red and black flags, in protest against the rejection of a bill for increasing the duty on imported silks. Troops were brought into London, the Riot Act was read, and serious civil disturbance was narrowly averted. Nor did the Rockingham Ministry, which came into office in July, inspire greater confidence than its predecessors. To the ladies and gentlemen who walked round and round the Rotunda these events were gloomy portents for the future. Troubles or at least changes were coming. But they can have had no inkling of the changes that were to be brought about in the lives of their descendants by a young Scots engineer who discovered that year a method of condensing steam in a vessel entirely separated from the cylinder.

Some of the fashionable gentlemen in the Rotunda had been taking to wearing their own hair, powdered of course. Soon only the old-fashioned, or professional gentlemen such as lawyers and physicians, would wear wigs. The peruke-makers were in great distress, and had petitioned the King that February, but several of them were wearing their own hair when they presented their petition, thus showing how vain it is to try to stop the march of fashion.

Mr. Fawcett, Senior, was among the singers at Ranelagh that summer. He was an articled pupil of Dr. Arne's, and sang some of the first songs written by James Hook at both Richmond and Ranelagh in 1765. Four years later his son, John Fawcett, was born. As will be seen hereafter, he also appeared at Ranelagh.

James Hook, whose name will recur often, was born at Norwich in 1746, and came to London very young. The songs for Richmond and Ranelagh were his Opus 1, and the greater part of his music was written for the Pleasure Gardens. He is said to have composed upwards of two thousand songs, besides catches and glees, some theatre music, and some chamber music. He also taught music at a school, where Mary Russell Mitford was his pupil, and was organist at St. John's, Harley-down. From 1774 to 1820 he composed for Vauxhall, and there are many volumes of his songs written for that place of entertainment. But he was almost as busy writing for Ranelagh. That many of his songs are pot-boilers, in which the same musical clichés appear again and again, is scarcely surprising. What is surprising is the freshness and grace of some of his melodies and his musical treatment of them. He was but a fourth-rate composer, perhaps, yet his melodic gift was outstanding, and he had a sense of word-value which made him an ideal Pleasure Gardens composer. He may sometimes be trite, but he is never vulgar. The good taste and elegance of his century are second nature to him, and he turned out his gracefully proportioned songs by the hundred, just as quite humble craftsmen who had read the *Gentlemen's and Cabinet-maker's Directory* turned out gracefully proportioned furniture. He was but a cunning musical craftsman, perhaps, but in the eighteenth century craftsmen were often artists. He died at Boulogne in 1827.

' The Venetians,' who performed instrumental music and ballads, usually in the Chinese Temple, were a new attraction in the 1765 season. Their first violin was Mr. Hay. Richard Hay was Master of the State Musick in Dublin 1767 – 1783.

Mr. Hudson, a popular but not outstanding Pleasure Gardens singer, was also heard that year.

* * *

The early summer of 1766 was wet and unfavourable to out-door entertainments. (So wet that the haymakers assembled on June 3rd outside the Royal Exchange, when a collection was made to compensate them for the work they had lost in the heavy rains.) But music and fireworks came back in June and July. The General Lying-in Hospital benefited from ' an elegant Set of Fire-Works ' arranged once more by Mr. Angelo, ' Who from Motives of Humanity and Generosity had obligingly undertaken the Conduct and Direction, as well as the Composition thereof, for the Benefit of that most excellent and useful Charity, which now greatly wants the Support and Assistance of the Public.'

This was the summer in which Isabella Young II, Mrs. Scott, sang in *Acis and Galatea* ; her uncle-in-law was still in charge of the music, with Mr. Hay as first violin. Pseudo-Scots songs continued to be popular, and a typical specimen sung at Ranelagh in 1766 was ' Betsy wilt thou gang with me ?,' of which the melody is well-sprinkled with Scots snaps.

Meanwhile, there were general rejoicings on the other side of the Atlantic at the repeal of the Stamp Act, and subscriptions were raised to erect statues to Mr. Pitt. Mr. Pitt formed a ministry that August and ceased to be Mr. Pitt; the Great Commoner accepted a peerage and became Earl of Chatham. The City and the mob were both angry, and he seemed to have lost much of his popularity. His health was undermined by gout, his judgment was impaired, and he had a mediocre team of ministers. The general uneasiness of the time was increased by news of riots in some parts of the country because of the dearness of provisions.

* * *

The fluctuations in Lord Chatham's health (in April the gout had flown up into his head), the divisions among his ministers, and the affairs of India and the American colonies were the chief topics of conversation in the summer of 1767. The Chancellor of the Exchequer introduced in June a resolution for imposing duties upon glass, paper, tea and other articles imported into America, which revived the dispute between ourselves and our colonies. The price of Parliamentary seats went up considerably this year, as the result of the high prices bid by the Nabobs returning from India. There was no such thing as a borough to be had under three thousand. In July Lord Clive, most splendid of the Nabobs, arrived in England with presents of diamonds for the King and Queen.

Meanwhile, the Arne clan continued to provide Ranelagh with music. On May 12th there was a grand performance of ' much-admired ' glees and catches taken from the collection of the Noblemen's and Gentlemen's Glee and Catch Club.

A generation which has rediscovered the Elizabethan madrigal, with all the richness and surprises of its contrapuntal writing, and the beauty of its poetry, is not likely to be impressed by the glee, progressing unadventurously from one decorous harmony to another, and frequently (though not always) making use of trivial verse. Yet, together with its more raffish brother, the catch, it played a big part in English musical life, both professional and amateur, in the last forty years of the eighteenth century and the first thirty of the nineteenth. Every professional male singer was expected to sing in a glee if required, were he bass, tenor or falsetto, while Glee and Catch Clubs sprang up all over the country at which amateurs, often with professional ' stiffening,' met to sing, drink and smoke at weekly or monthly intervals. The most famous of these was the Noblemen's and Gentlemen's Glee and Catch Club, founded in 1761, which included both professional and amateur members. Among the amateurs were many members of the royal family and of the peerage. The rules required members to take the chair in turn, and the Club met every Tuesday from

February to June at the Thatched House Tavern, except during Passion and Easter weeks.

Because of the size of the Rotunda, the glees were performed on this occasion, May 12th, 1767, with choral parts and an instrumental accompaniment, both composed by Dr. Arne. Six choirboys, Mrs. Arne (lately Miss Wright, now the wife of Michael Arne), and Miss Frederic (a pupil of Dr. Arne) sang the treble parts. The catches were led by Vernon, Champness, Dibdin and Parsons.

Vernon was principal tenor at Vauxhall from 1764 – 1781, and popular at the theatres also, where he sang the usual tenor repertoire of the day. Bell's ' British Theatre ' gives a dashing portrait of him as Macheath, but Cooke considers he was too much of the coxcomb and not enough of the highwayman in the part. Lee Lewes describes him as ' one of the most popular ornaments, both as an actor and a singer, the London stage had to boast for a series of years ... His judgment was correct, his execution rapid, and his expression such as went to every heart.' Other contemporaries speak of his ' gay and energetic manner,' and his ' exquisite taste.' A romantic tale is told of his ' discovery.' Yates and Palmer were stopping at the Bull Inn, Coventry, on their way to open their theatre at Birmingham, when they heard a poor lad singing in the street to earn support for his widowed mother. Yates had the boy apprenticed to himself, and educated him, later handing him over to Garrick ' for a valuable consideration.' Garrick had him instructed in ' music, dancing, fencing, etc,' and brought him out on the stage. His name is associated more especially with Vauxhall, but we shall meet with him again at Ranelagh. He composed at least one song which is still sung, a setting of the Clown's Song in *Twelfth Night*.

Champness has already been mentioned. Charles Dibdin is remembered by most people as the composer of ' Tom Bowling,' ' The Lass that loves a Sailor,' ' Farewell, my trim-built

L

wherry,' and other ballads, but he was a singer as well as a
composer, and that is probably one of the reasons why his
songs are so singable. He was born at Southampton in 1745,
and was a chorister at Winchester under Fussell. When he was
fourteen he tried and failed to obtain a post as organist at
Waltham in Hampshire, and then came to London to join his
sailor brother, who gave him useful introductions to ' city
friends.' These gentlemen patronised him for a time, he tells
us, and then neglected him because he rebelled at being
treated as a mere buffoon, ready to entertain the company
gratis when required. For a while he tuned harpsichords for
Johnson, a music-seller in Cheapside, and probably helped in
the shop. He tried his hand at composition, and sold the copy-
right of six ballads to Thompson, of St. Paul's, Cheapside, for
three guineas. They were sung by Mr. Kear at Finch's Grotto
Gardens, and sold for 1½d. each. Meanwhile, his brother had
gone to sea and been taken prisoner by the French, so that he
was left entirely to his own resources until he obtained an
introduction to Covent Garden. He was first engaged as a
chorus singer, but on May 21st, 1764, he appeared as Strephon
in *The Shepherd's Artifice*, a pastoral of which he had composed
both words and music. But he had not forgotten his Cathedral
training, and in those early days he used to play the organ at
St. Bride's, Fleet Street, introducing ' Lilliburlero ' and other
secular melodies into his voluntaries. The year after *The Shepherd's Artifice* he was such a success as Ralph in Samuel
Arnold's ballad opera *The Maid of the Mill* that ' Ralph
handkerchiefs ' were worn in his honour. By the summer of
1767 he was well established as singer and composer, although
his most successful ' operas,' *The Padlock* and *Lionel and
Clarissa*, did not come out until the next year.

Parsons, who must have sung alto in the quartet, not to be
confused with Parsons the actor, was what might be termed a
' useful ' singer, scarcely more.

A Glee Elegiac may seem a contradiction in terms, but Mr. Norris composed one for this occasion, in memory of the truly wise virtuous and valiant commander, sometimes less politely called Butcher Cumberland. The words were as follows :–

> *O'er William's tomb, with love and grief opprest,*
> *Britannia mourns her hero now at rest ;*
> *Not tears alone, but praises too she gives,*
> *Due to the Guardian of our laws and lives.*
> *Nor shall the laurel ever fade with years,*
> *Whose leaves are water'd with a nation's tears.*

The nation's tears must have dried rather rapidly, for Cumberland's laurels faded within a very few years.

This programme of glees was repeated at Drury Lane the following year. Fireworks continued, and two ' Italian Games ' were exhibited on the canal, called ' La Giostra ' and ' La Corsa del Palio.' (*sic*)

At other Ranelagh concerts Mr. Hay played concertos on the violin, and Mr. Baildon concertos on the organ.

There were attempts at enforcing traffic regulations that summer. The Nobility and Gentry were earnestly requested to order their Coachmen to ' keep to the Right of the Road from Town, and also down the Avenue, and not to order their Carriages up to the Doors until they are ready to go away, as the Coaches cannot be suffered to stand at the Doors, but must (if their Company is not ready) drive off.' There was a ' Guard on Horseback to patrol the Roads until the Company was gone ' each night. Highway robbery continued.

* * *

Two familiar Ranelagh figures would not be seen in the Rotunda in the 1768 season. *The Sentimental Journey* had been published at the end of February, and on March 18th Laurence Sterne died in Bond Street. Bonnell Thornton, author of the *Burlesque Ode*, died on May 9th. There had been strikes and riots in the early spring, following a bad winter, and then a general election, in the course of which the Wilkes affair had revived. Wilkes had come over from his exile on the Continent, and applied for a pardon, but his application was disregarded. He offered himself as a parliamentary candidate first for the City of London, where he was last on the poll, and then for Middlesex, which returned him with a large majority. He was ordered into custody, rescued by an enthusiastic mob, surrendered himself, and was securely lodged in the King's Bench prison when Parliament met on May 10th. His followers, crying ' Wilkes and Liberty ! ' tried to carry him in triumph to the House of Commons. When they were prevented a riot ensued. The mob suffered nobody to pass unless they were wearing blue cockades, and papers inscribed ' No. 45 Wilkes and Liberty ! ' People were forced to illuminate their houses.

To distract patrons from all these disturbances, Mrs. (Michael) Arne, Mrs. Barthelemon (Polly Young), Mr. Champness and Mr. Raworth, a tenor little known to fame, with chorus, sang :

> *A Truce with Elections, and Politics too,*
> *What have we with their bustle and nonsense to do ?*
> *This Dome was the Temple of Concord design'd,*
> *Of innocent Mirth and of Pleasure refin'd,*
> *And I am a priestess attending the Fane*
> *And will not be called to the office in vain.*
> *Come, come then away, ye young and ye gay,*
> *Set joy on the wing, for what month in the spring ;*
> *Is so lively and merry as May ?*

Songs composed by F. Barthelemon sung by his wife and ' Master Blundell ' that year at Ranelagh were to be obtained of the author at Mr. Howel's, silk mercer, in Marybone Street

Golden Square, or at Welcker's Music Shop, Gerrard Street, Soho. Michael Arne composed this year a Song and Chorus, the words by David Garrick, Esq.

Riots continued all that summer, some originating in the Wilkes affair, and others in wages disputes. People were frequently assaulted in the streets, and Ranelagh continued to provide a horse guard to patrol the approach roads.

Another excitement that year was the visit to this country of His Majesty King Christian VII of Denmark, who had married Princess Caroline Mathilda, sister of George III. (Three years later he divorced her.) He was small of stature, nineteen years of age, with a pale delicate face, and looked to Horace Walpole like a fairy-tale prince who had just come out of the kernel of a nut. A new apartment had been furnished for him at St. James's at the cost of £3,000, and it was said his table cost his royal brother-in-law no less than £84 a day, exclusive of wine. He planned to give a splendid masked ball to ' the Nobility &c ' at his own expense in the early autumn at Ranelagh. The Proprietors waited on his Danish Majesty to discuss the subject, but the Opera House was chosen instead, it being considered rather late in the year for Ranelagh. He visited the Rotunda, however, as he visited the opera and all the other entertainments of London, and early in September, Ranelagh honoured him with a ' magnificent piece of fireworks, to conclude with an Illuminated Structure forty feet high, decorated suitable to the occasion.' George III's birthday had been similarly honoured in June, when Handel's Music for the Royal Fireworks had been revived.

*   *   *

When the 1769 season opened, the promenaders were still talking of Wilkes, his elections and counter-elections. Affairs in America seemed more unsatisfactory than ever, and the coercive policy of the King and Lord North was far from

universally approved. ' Iphigenia ' had married the Duke of
Kingston in March ; she had grown tired of waiting for Lord
Bristol to die, and swore she was a spinster, in spite of that
little matter of the Church register at Lainston.

On May 12th at a *bal paré* and Jubilee Ridotto, Charles
Dibdin produced his ' new Musical Entertainment in the
manner of the Italian Comic Serenatas, call'd THE EPHES-
IAN MATRON with words by Mr. Bickerstaffe.' It was
repeated several times that season, as part of the usual evening's entertainment – it lasted about an hour – and shared the
programme with elegant fireworks, and music performed in
the Garden orchestra or in the boats on the canal. (It was also
given at the Little Haymarket Theatre on August 31st.)

The Ephesian Matron herself, whose resolution to die in her
husband's tomb is so quickly shaken, was sung by Mrs. Sophia
Baddeley, as famous for her intrigues as for her beauty. Her
father was Valentine Snow, Sergeant Trumpeter to the King,
who played Handel's trumpet solos, and she must have had
some musical background as well as a sweet voice, and a certain amount of training. When she was eighteen she eloped
with the actor, Baddeley, and soon after appeared on the stage.
She was what was called a ' singing actress,' rather than a
singer, and it seems likely she would never have made much
headway as actress or singer without her personal charms. In
genteel comedy such as *The Clandestine Marriage* she charmed
her audience into thinking she could act, and her singing seems
to have been at least ' agreeable.' When she came on to the
stage at Bath as Polly on one occasion, Dr. Herschel, who was
playing violin in the orchestra, dropped his bow and gazed at
her beauty in astonishment. She was an ideal heroine for
ballad operas or serenatas, and the Pleasure Gardens were a
suitable setting for her charms. The *Town and Country Magazine* was probably not exaggerating when it described her as
' amongst those fickle fair ones, who consider constancy as a

vice, and fidelity in love as a crime.' The general view was that
Mr. Baddeley condoned his wife's infidelities for mercenary
reasons, although he did fight one duel on her account.
' Beauty will ever command admirers, and the husbands who
do not pay a due devotion to the shrine, must expect the
ladies will receive their expected adulation from other votaries,' considered the gossip-writer. Mrs. Baddeley, too, had a
love of jewellery and of every kind of luxury, which the other
votaries seem to have been able and ready to supply.

The Maid in *The Ephesian Matron*, a typical impertinent
soubrette, was taken by Mrs. Thompson, who was a Pleasure
Gardens singer of some note, though not in the first rank. The
next year she sang Serpina in *La Serva Padrona* at Marylebone
Gardens, as well as in Dibdin's Ranelagh productions. Charles
Dibdin himself was the Centurion who consoles the Matron so
speedily, and Mr. Legg – a singing actor on the pay-roll of
Covent Garden, and a performer at Marylebone Gardens –
was the father.

The ' Advertisement,' *i.e.*, preface, to the libretto of *The
Ephesian Matron* tells us what Dibdin had in mind when he
introduced these serenatas at Ranelagh :

' Those who are acquainted with Italian musical compositions, must know, that there are among them many short
comic dramas (a longer sort of cantatas) where little fables are
pursued ; such as La Serva Padrona, Baioco e Serpilla, Lo
Maestro di Cappella &c.

' It has been suggested to the managers of RANELAGH,
by a gentleman long presiding with unrival'd talents, over the
most capital of our public entertainments ; that something in
the same way would be an improvement upon the detached
songs and ballads, usually sung in their orchestra. In deference
to his judgment, this is an Essay.

' It would be needless to observe that the words are to be no
farther considered than as they are adapted, and serve to give

stile and character to the music. But should the music, when it has been sufficiently heard to render it somewhat familiar, be found pleasing enough to make the entertainment, on the whole, agreeable to the public, other pieces may be written much more pardonable, than what had here, at a short warning, been in great haste put together.'

The gentleman who presided with unrivalled talents over Ranelagh was, presumably, Sir Thomas Robinson.

The company which heard the first performance of *The Ephesian Matron* is described as ' very brilliant,' and included H.R.H. the Duke of Cumberland (Henry Frederick, brother of George III, born in 1745 about the time his uncle and namesake was winning in Scotland those laurels later to be watered by a nation's tears), and H.R.H. the Duke of Gloucester (another brother of George III, born 1743). Both of them made marriages which were not recognised at court, the former to Mrs. Horton, and the latter to Horace Walpole's lovely niece, Lady Waldegrave.

The Chinese Temple and other parts of the Gardens were illuminated, a large sea horse stuck full of small lamps floated on the canal, and over the canal itself was an illuminated arch. The Rotunda was also very elegantly illuminated with several thousand wax lights. Unfortunately, however, the refreshments were not sufficiently abundant to please the company early in the evening ; several gentlemen broke into the wine cellar and helped themselves. Later in the evening plenty of wine and sweets were available, and Sir Thomas Robinson, to smooth ruffled tempers, asked the company to sup with him. This provoked some criticism. *The Ephesian Matron* was performed at ten o'clock, about midnight there was dancing, and the party did not break up till nearly four in the morning. Not all the company appeared in ' fancied dresses,' but among those who did were a Sultana dressed in crimson sattin (*sic*) trimmed with silver, and a Spaniard in yellow trimmed with black, and a great number of diamonds in his hat. One lady lost on this occasion what was probably a precious keepsake, ' a bracelet of black velvet, with the Picture of a Sea-officer in his uniform,' and we hope that some honest person found it and brought it back to Mr. Davis, book-seller in Piccadilly. Who was the painter of this miniature ? Mr. Jeremiah Meyer, perhaps. Another lady lost a crescent from her headdress, consisting of seven brilliants, and a small star of five brilliants in the middle. Perhaps this was worn by the Sultana.

Thieves were not unknown even inside the Gardens, and the Horse Patrol on the road was still necessary. A new danger threatened Ranelagh patrons : ' The Company that come by Hyde Park Corner are requested to order their Carriages to keep the Turnpike Road by Pimlico, to prevent accidents that must unavoidably happen by going down the Descent of the New Road by the Fire Engine.' The footway from Buckingham Gate had been lately mended and enlarged, however, so that it was very safe and easy for those who preferred to come by sedan chair.

On June 9th Ranelagh gave ' An Assembly ' for the benefit of the Middlesex Hospital (founded in 1745), which provided a concert, fireworks on the canal and a ball for half a guinea.

*　　　*　　　*

Dibdin's ' essay ' was sufficiently appreciated to encourage him to produce another serenata in 1770, *The Recruiting Sergeant*, with vocal parts again by himself, Mrs. Baddeley and Mrs. Thompson, and Charles Bannister as bass in place of Mr. Legg. Charles Bannister had been launched on the London stage in 1762. He had a remarkable deep bass voice, which he often abandoned for a very high falsetto. ' Old Bannister had voice enough but not a particle of science, and did wonders without it,' said Boaden. He seems, indeed, to have been a self-taught singer, with a musical ear and a talent for mimicry which was a great asset at a period when ' imitations ' were popular. He probably picked up a certain amount of voice production and style from the singers he imitated. That an untrained bass voice of rich quality and wide range should stir an audience in such ditties as ' Brave Admiral Benbow ' and ' Stand to your guns ' is not surprising. That he should use both his bass voice and his falsetto to imitate with success Champness, Tenducci, and other well-known singers, shows that he had a parrot-like gift for reproducing the tones which his quick ear perceived. Garrick first engaged him for Merlin, a bass role, in *Cymon* in 1767, and from then until 1782 he played constantly at Drury Lane. Caliban was one of his favourite parts, and also Hecate, which had been sung by old Leveridge before him. (Lee Lewes says he was told that Bannister was an illegitimate son of old Leveridge, but I have found no corroboration of this). His ' Steady ' in *The Quaker* was said to be unrivalled, and he played Polly in the curious travestied *Beggar's Opera*. Anthony Pasquin speaks of him thus :-

> *In thunder harmonious his cadences roll,*
> *And the full tide of melody pours on the soul ;*
> *His tones, the cold breast of frigidity warming,*
> *Are audible, sonorous, manly and charming.*

He was well known as a wit and a good fellow, expensive reputations to keep up, and prudence in money-matters was not in his nature, so that in later years he was dependent on his son Jack. When he earned £6 a week, he explained, it was easy to keep out of debt, because it was paid to him every Saturday night on the Treasurer's table, but when he earned £15, and had to wait for it, he would live on credit, and pile up debts in the meanwhile. (Many other people besides Charles Bannister have found it easier to live within the bounds of a small weekly salary than within the bounds of one much larger paid monthly or quarterly.) He did not retire, finally, until the

1799 – 1800 season, and one of the most memorable benefits of his career was that of November 17th, 1800, just after the Battle of the Nile, when Nelson and the Hamiltons were present. That the one-time singer of so many stirring sea-songs should thus appear in public with the Victor of the Nile was considered ' very affecting.'

But in the summer of 1770 none of that could have been foreseen. The future Lord Nelson was twelve years old, and Jack Bannister, beloved of Hazlitt and Charles Lamb, was only ten.

In June an English version of *La Serva Padrona* was given, but in spite of the success of the 'serenatas,' 'detached songs and ballads' were still sung, and the Scots song continued to be popular. We find a young lady called Miss Sharpe telling us that:–

> *By the side of the sweet river Tay,*
> *Or else on the banks of the Tweed,*
> *Young Colin he whistles all day,*
> *Or merrily pipes on his reed.*

*　　　*　　　*

In 1770 began that change in hairdressing which was to lead to such extravagances by the middle of the decade. The neat close hairdressing, which had been worn with various modifications by ladies ever since Ranelagh opened, disappeared, and heads grew higher and higher. The hair was frizzed and stretched over frames of wire, greased and powdered, and surmounted with some arrangement of flowers, fruit, or even model ships. Samuel Rogers once went to Ranelagh with a lady who was obliged to sit on a stool in the bottom of the coach, the height of her headdress not allowing her to occupy the regular seat. But in 1770 the fashion for high heads was only beginning. There was a brief period when gentlemen's heads also rose skywards, and they wore padded toupets which rose sharply from the forehead. But this did not last long. The waistcoats worn at Ranelagh were particularly decorative.

Ranelagh waistcoats and Ranelagh silks were advertised. Here are advertisements of 1770 which give some idea of the variety of colours and fabrics used :—

'A large and elegant Assortment in Gold, Silver and Colours, and some beautiful Patterns in Colours only ; great variety worked with the Tambour on Silk, Sattin, Callico, Muslin etc., great choice of Manchester Brocades in Gold and Silver of the newest and most admired Patterns ; likewise a new discovered Gold coloured Silk worked on muslin for Ladies and Gentlemen's Wear ; it is dyed from an actual Solution of Gold by a Chymical Process, and has the peculiar Property of receiving additional Beauty by washing ; it is particularly calculated for the warmer Climates where Gold by Perspiration is so liable to tarnish. Merchants and Captains trading to the West Indies may be supplied with any Quantity at the shortest notice, and good Allowance to the Trade, and those who make them up, at J. Smith's, Number 49, the Corner of Serjeant's Inn, Fleet Street.'

'Silver Ranelagh Silks in various Patterns, by the original Manufacturer, at the Coventry Cross in Chandos Street, Covent Garden; also Lustrings and other fashionable silks of entire new Fancies, adapted for the present Season at very low Rates.' *The Macaroni and Theatrical Magazine* gives the following fashion news for gentlemen in 1772 :

'Hats rising behind and falling before, the blazing gold loop, the full-moon button, together with the triple row of binding round the crown, are totally exploded, and succeeded by a single narrow looping, broad hat-band, and pin's head button ; the single buckle (i.e. curl) on each side the head still continues in undress ; in full dress, the three buckles zig zag, with the foretop *à la grecque* ; the roses are entirely confined to the upside, and the bags (i.e. bag-wigs) encreasing every day.

'The late stunting of the coats has promoted the growth of the skirts ; the pockets of which are at present in a capacity

The Lovely Sacarissa Dressing for the Rotunda!

of holding conveniently a tolerable sized muslin handkerchief
and smelling bottle.

' Shoes decreased in heels two inches ; low-quartered and
sharp-pointed, and cut like a butter-boat to show the whole of
the clock of the stocking, which is of a different coloured silk ;
it is thought, however, that this fashion will not hold long, as
macaronis have been confined to their rooms with sore throats,
in consequence of their taking cold in that quarter.'

*   *   *

Our relations with the American colonies seemed to be going from bad to worse in the summer of 1771. The Wilkes
affair continued to convulse the nation, the Commons and the
City of London were at open war, and Lord North was pro-
digiously hissed on his way to the House of Commons at the
end of March. The once popular young King was alienating
the affections of many of his subjects by his obstinacy and fixed
ideas; the cabinet system established by Sir Robert Walpole
was in eclipse, and George III was virtually Prime Minister.

But Ranelagh loyally celebrated his birthday, this time with
a firework by Mr. François Caillot, and the regular musical
entertainments continued. Charles Dibdin, Charles Bannister,
Mrs. Baddeley and Mrs. Thompson were singing, and a concerto was played on the organ by Dr. Burney, who had returned from his first foreign tour at the end of the previous
year. Among visitors to Ranelagh that summer were Dr. Goldsmith and Sir Joshua Reynolds, who had painted Goldsmith's
portrait the year before, Fanny Burney, and some distinguished foreigners, including the Duc de la Trémouille. But
some of Ranelagh's first patrons had already disappeared.
That August, Thomas Gray died.

The ' no-parking ' order had had no effect, apparently, and
the Proprietors issued another appeal : ' As several Ladies and
Gentlemen order their Carriages at a particular Time, such

Ladies and Gentlemen are requested to be in Readiness to go at the Time appointed, to prevent the great Inconveniency which arises from the Servants insisting they were ordered, and that they would not move till their Company came.'

*   *   *

The lovely Mrs. Baddeley was still singing at Ranelagh in 1772, and there were the usual concerts of vocal and instrumental music, with interludes of wind music ' between the Acts.' The firework on July 18th was universally allowed to be ' one of the most capital exhibitions ever seen in this kingdom. The company, for the season of the year, was extreamly (*sic*) numerous, and contained persons of the first distinction.' The ' litterary people ' included Mr. Garrick, Dr. Goldsmith and Dr. Johnson. Dr. Johnson often went to Ranelagh, which he deemed ' a place of innocent recreation,' but it inspired gloomy reflections. ' When I first entered Ranelagh,' he said ' it gave an expansion and gay sensation to my mind, such as I never experienced anywhere else. But, as Xerxes wept when he viewed his immense army, and considered that not one of that great multitude would be alive a hundred years afterwards, so it went to my heart to consider that there was not one in all that brilliant circle that was not afraid to go home and think ; but that the thoughts of each individual there, would be distressing when alone.' Among the music they heard performed by the band that evening was ' the soul-inspiring War Piece called the BATTLE OF PRAGUE.'

That April 1st one of the last of the rebels' heads on Temple Bar fell down. Of the grim row people had gaped at in 1746, only one now remained – a black, shapeless lump.

*   *   *

Political events in the eighteenth century moved at what seems to us a very slow tempo. Tension between ourselves and the Colonies continued through the early 1770's, but it took a long time before breaking-point was reached. Indian politics were also disturbing. Some people began to be uneasy in their minds as to how the Nabobs acquired all those diamonds and riches with which they returned to England. On May 7th, 1773, however, the Commons resolved that Robert, Lord Clive, although he had wrongfully possessed himself of £234,000 by an abuse of the power with which he was entrusted in India, had yet rendered great service to his country. Meanwhile, balls, fireworks and concerts, continued at Ranelagh, and fashions grew more and more extravagant as we approached catastrophe. It was the age of the Macaroni with his high toupet and enormous nosegay and his quizzing glass. The impertinent macaroni would approach his glass quite close to the features of any lady he admired in the Rotunda. A writer in the *London Magazine* would have liked to break every coxcomb's glass that was directed ' in an offensive manner against the eye, the cheek or the lip of hallowed virtue.' The ladies' weapon at that period was the fan, which became more and more exquisite in workmanship, often with sticks of delicately carved ivory and tiny scenes painted on the silk by the best artists.

In the early 70's the fashionable people came late to Ranelagh ; they would ' come in about eleven, stare about them for half an hour, laugh at the other fools who are drenching and scalding themselves with coffee and tea.' But the ' citizens ' came early, in order not to miss anything. Some worthy citizens' wives insisted on their husbands wearing swords, which were difficult to manage in a crowd unless you were accustomed to them. ' Some turn the hilt behind, and the point forward, which is for ever entangled with the train of some lady's trailing frock. Some for fear of double misfortune to their toes, as well as their toasting irons, hold their swords straight, and turn their toes in.'

The *chapeau bras* required as careful management as the sword. Hats were not often worn at this period, but were carried under the arm ; indeed, they would have had to be very large indeed to go over the high wigs, and so fashion decreed they should be very small. A country boor did not know 'which arm he was to put it under, sometimes he had it in his hand, and often betrayed a great inclination to put it on his head, concluding it was a damned, troublesome useless thing, and a man might as well be without it.'

A bag wig, too, was often 'a very troublesome appendage to a man's head. A person unused to it will be immediately detected, because he will jerk his head this way or that, next feeling if it is on, for the shortness of the hair keeps the mind in perpetual alarm ; and if it falls off, which is not an uncommon case, the confusion is compleated, and the unbagged gentlemen is under the disagreeable necessity of pocketing his foppery, and making his retreat.' (It will be seen from this that ' to unbag ' in the eighteenth century did not mean the same as ' to debag ' means in the twentieth.)

There were still rose-sellers outside the entrance to Ranelagh, as there had been in 1746 when Lord Cholmondeley thought himself so insulted. In the early summer of 1774 a recently returned nabob who was ' engaged with three ladies on a party to Ranelagh ' politely presented a rose to each of the three ladies, keeping one for himself, and gave the flower-girl sixpence. ' God bless your honor, they are half a crown each ! ' she protested. ' What ! *Half a crown* for a rose ? ' ' Yes your honor, at this time of the year.' ' You impudent hussy, give me my sixpence back ! ' And the three ladies had to hand back their roses to the flower-girl. It was the custom a little later for gentlemen to buy in the anteroom nosegays of myrtles, hyacinths or roses to present to their ladies. The macaronis themselves often carried nosegays.

1774 was a glorious summer, and the promenaders had two

M

weddings among the great folk to talk about – that of the Duke
of Devonshire to Lady Georgiana Spencer, and that of Lord
Stanley to Lady Elizabeth Hamilton, which last was celebrated by a famous *fête champêtre* at the Oaks, Epsom. That
fête nearly eclipsed all Ranelagh's diversions, and made people
forget even the outrage of the Boston Tea Party. ('Mrs. Britannia orders her Senate to proclaim America a continent of
cowards, and vote it should be starved unless it will drink tea
with her, ' was Walpole's comment.)

In 1774 Ranelagh nearly lost its chief shareholder, ' that
Maypole and garland of May delights,' Sir Thomas Robinson ;
he was seized with a violent fever, but was ' thoroughly recovered by taking only two doses of Dr. James's Powder.' Dr.
James's Powder was the universal panacea of the period ;
Horace Walpole believed it would cure everything ' but the
villainies of physicians.' But it did not save Dr. Goldsmith – in
fact some people thought it killed him. In spite of all his
apothecary would say, Goldsmith would dose himself with
these powders when he developed a nervous fever at the end of
March, ' after which he became worse and worse,' according
to the opponents of Dr. James's, and died on April 4th in
Brick Court, Temple.

*   *   *

The crisis came at last. The summer of 1775 was a kind of
1914. Before us was a war which was to last seven years and
bring us to the verge of disaster, followed by eight years of
uneasy peace, before the longest struggle of our history – a
struggle not to be decided until many years after Ranelagh,
together with many other eighteenth-century institutions, had
been swept away. 1775 was the high tide of eighteenth-century
social life, and the high tide of fantastic fashions.

War was now inevitable, for although some of the wisest
men of the age opposed the policy of Lord North and the King,

the Opposition was too weak to check it. News came slowly
and uncertainly from America, and meanwhile London
amused itself, and music flourished exceedingly. On a Saturday in March you could take your choice of a Bach and Abel
concert, the Italian Opera House, Drury Lane, Covent Garden or Ranelagh. Garrick was still acting. Dr. Johnson and
Boswell were back from the Hebrides. At dawn on May Day
boys and girls went out to the tea-gardens of Marylebone or
Kentish Town to eat hot rolls and buns, and later the chimney
sweepers whitened their faces and danced in the streets with
the milkmaids and milkmen. That night Mr. Sheridan's *St.
Patrick's Day* was produced with success at Covent Garden.
Horace Walpole decided he must leave to the younger generation the learning of the map of America ; after all, it would be
their business.

Ranelagh opened with the usual vocal and instrumental
concerts, and on June 23rd, six days after the Battle of Bunkers
Hill, took place the most brilliant and novel entertainment of
its history ; The Ranelagh Regatta and Ball.

*   *   *

Whenever a new kind of entertainment was introduced in
the eighteenth century, people liked to be assured either that
there was a good precedent for it in classical times, or else that
it could be justified on moral grounds. They liked to feel that
their least action had its place in an ordered universe, that every
novelty had a respectable pedigree. A plausible reason must be
found even for amusing oneself. A regatta was a new form of
entertainment for the Thames, and therefore the author of 'A
Circumstantial Account of the Ensuing Regatta ' – a pamphlet intended to form ' An Agreeable Companion ' to the
spectators of this elegant diversion – was at pains to show how
right and proper it was from every point of view.

After a passing allusion to the games of ancient Greece and

the bullfights of Spain, he examines in measured prose ' the
public entertainments peculiar to this land ' – such as operas,
theatrical representations and masquerades – concluding that
' of all public entertainments those which deserve most to be
advanced in Great Britain, are Naval Sports and Exercises,
such as Rowing, Sailing &c.' He then discusses the origins of
the word ' regatta,' and describes the regattas of Venice. From
Venice he moves to the amusements of ' the polite Romans '
in the reign of Augustus, thence to Gower's account of meeting Henry IV and his court upon the river Thames, and thence
to more recent examples of Royal patronage of ' entertainments of this kind upon the water.'

Having satisfactorily established both that this entertainment is of ancient lineage and that it has a moral, even a patriotic, purpose, the author explains that it owes its inception to
the Scavoir Vivre Club. He considers that it must ' give the
greatest pleasure to every lover of his country, to find, that,
while this unhappy nation is distracted by party-feuds, there
are found so many respectable noblemen, and gentlemen, of
truly patriotic principles, and whose abilities do honour to the
sphere they move in, who prefer the solid pleasure of finding
employment for the labouring mechanic, to the ideal satisfaction of signalising themselves in the cabals of state, or courting
the acclamations of a giddy and intoxicated mob.' He laments
that the noblemen and gentlemen who constitute the Scavoir
Vivre, Boodle's, Almack's and Goosetree's ' have been cruelly
insulted by the snarlings of malevolence, the ravings of enthusiasm (i.e., the followers of Wesley and Whitfield, and other
' dissenters '), and the wretched cant of fanatics of almost
every denomination ; instead of receiving that applause and
commendation they are so justly entitled to, for their patriotic endeavours to promote the trade and manufactures of
this country.'

The author now explains ' the Plan of the Regatta.' From

ten in the morning until noon of the great day, the bells of St.
Margaret's, Westminster, will ring, and the company are to
embark at the several stairs adjacent to Westminster Bridge
between six and seven in the evening. Only 1,300 tickets are to
be issued, and these only to members of the clubs already
mentioned. The barges belonging to the Lord Mayor and City
Companies will accommodate a good number of the subscribers ; others will be in private barges or boats, of which the
rowers must be ' uniformly dressed,' and must show one of the
' three marine colours ' white, blue or red. The Marshal's
barge of twelve oars, carrying a blue standard, and the word
REGATTA in large gold characters, is to be ' stationed to the
westward of the centre arch ; the rest of the boats and barges
to spread out at such distances on the rendezvous as to fill all
the arches of Westminster Bridge at once,' leaving the centre
arch free for the twelve race boats ' each rowed by two young
watermen, who have come out of their apprenticeship since
June 1772,' who were to row round a vessel moored off Waterman's Hall near London Bridge, whence they were to return to
Westminster. The first three boats to clear the centre arch
would receive the following prizes : ' First men to have ten
guineas each, with Coats and Badges ; Second Men – Seven
Guineas each, with Coats and Badges of an inferior value :
Third Men – Five Guineas each, with Coats and Badges of less
value than the second.' Every successful waterman would have
an ensign given to him to wear that year on the Thames, ' with
the word REGATTA in gold letters thereon, inscribed with 1,
2 or 3, according to the order in which he may arrive at the
close of the race.'

After the race, the whole procession would move up the
river to Ranelagh. ' Three military bands of music, composed
of fifes, drums, cymbals etc, would be habited in a manner
consonant to the naval flags of Great Britain, and be properly
stationed, as will likewise three other select bands, of the most

eminent masters on wind instruments, all under such regulations as may best entertain the company while on the water, and at the time of disembarking.' The platform of Chelsea Hospital was to be open ' for the greater conveniency of the Ladies and Gentlemen disembarking,' and the sailing boats on the river were to draw up in the form of a crescent facing Ranelagh Stairs.

The doors of the Rotunda would be thrown open at eleven o'clock, where circular ranges of tables were to be placed ' in such a manner as to form a magnificent amphitheatre (pyradimically (sic) rising towards the center, and terminating in an orchestra),' where the company would be served with a supper provided by the famed Mrs. Cornelys, and listen to music by 120 of the most celebrated vocal and instrumental performers in Great Britain, including Giardini and Fisher, who would perform ' solo pieces, solos, solo concertos ' and catches and glees. There would be more music in the Gardens, and in an ' antique amphitheatre ' on the edge of the canal – ninety-six feet in length and ninety feet wide, which communicated with the Rotunda by covered arcades – a choice band of musicians ' in sylvan dresses ' would play minuets, cotillions, and country dances. If the ladies and gentlemen choose to appear in fancy dress so much the better. It is expected, in any case, that most of the ladies will be dressed in white as ' the first mourning ' (for the divorced and exiled Queen of Denmark, who had recently died) will be out on the day before the Regatta. This will give ' an uniformity and most agreeable appearance to the whole scene.'

*   *   *

In spite of the laudable reasons for holding a regatta given at the beginning of the pamphlet, various objections have been made to it, which the author now refutes. It has been suggested that it will keep many of the nobility and gentry in London, which may benefit the trade of the metropolis, but be temporarily detrimental to summer resorts such as Tonbridge. But on the other hand, it will keep in England many ' who under the specious appearance of travelling for the benefit of their health, squander their fortunes in Gallic and Transalpine extravagance.' Surely Tonbridge will not mind losing a little to London in such a good cause as keeping the nobility and gentry away from France and Italy. It has even been suggested in some quarters that this polite entertainment was deliberately planned to prevent the nobility and gentry from attending the coronation of Louis XVI.

Another objection is the perennial one : tradesmen and labourers will be called from their respective employments, and the poorer sort of people encouraged to ' indulge their propensity to idleness.' But ' seasonable holidays,' considers our author – who has an answer to everything – are not destructive of morals ; on the contrary, ' the hard-working man, after his holiday, returns to his employment with high spirits, an alacrity of disposition and recruited strength.'

The patriotic theme is again introduced. The very existence of this nation depends in a great measure upon her fleet, and ' next to the vast body of mariners employed in the British fishery, the watermen on the river Thames constitute the greatest nursery for seamen to man the fleet.'

Doubtless many of the spectators of this elegant diversion read the ' Agreeable Companion ' during the tedious hours of waiting for the races to begin, and enjoyed themselves all the more for being convinced that they were taking part in something highly moral, patriotic and public-spirited.

* * *

The Regatta came off more or less according to the ' circumstantial plan,' though there were some modifications. The bells of St. Martin's rang in the morning, and those of St. Margaret's

about 8.30, the whole procession began to move towards Ranelagh.

*   *   *

Among the favoured subscribers who finished the day's festivities at Ranelagh were the Dukes of Gloucester and Cumberland, many of the nobility and gentry and the foreign ambassadors, but Horace Walpole was not among them. By eighteenth-century standards he was growing an old gentleman – he was 58 – and by 11 p.m. he was writing to Lady Upper Ossory, vowing that he would go to see no more sights, and pitying the rest of the company who would be ' stewing at Ranelagh.' Three hundred tickets had been made out to admit by land to Ranelagh such persons as were ' timorous, or do not chuse to appear upon water,' and these landlubbers must have had a splendid view of the approaching procession.

Predictions as to the splendidness of Mrs. Cornelys' supper were not fulfilled ; it was ' indifferent, and the wine very scarce.' Poor weather spoilt the illuminations in the Gardens. But in every other respect the polite entertainment seems to have surpassed expectations.

The sole complaint against the music was that the orchestra was the only part of the Rotunda not brilliantly illuminated by parti-coloured lamps, and so presented a gloomy appearance. Of the quality of the music itself – vocal and instrumental – there was no doubt.

Felice de Giardini led the orchestra. He came from Italy about 1750, and his beautiful tone and brilliance of execution completely eclipsed the playing of Michael Festing. Like other violinists (Geminiani, for instance, already mentioned as the singing-master of Cecilia Young I), he also taught singing. At one time he held morning concerts at his house, when his scholars, both vocal and instrumental, performed. When Michael Festing died in 1752, Giardini took his place as leader of the Italian Opera Orchestra, with excellent results, and at

MR. VERNON

one time he undertook the management of the opera as well, at
which he was less successful. In his turn, Giardini was to be
ousted from popular favour by Cramer, and we shall hear of
him again at Ranelagh in the sad days of his decline. But in
1775 he was still one of the most important figures in London
musical life.   Fisher was associated with him on the occasion
of the Regatta concert. This was probably John Abraham
Fisher, a well-known violinist and composer of theatre music,
born in 1744. His marriage Miss to Powell, daughter of the

actor, brought him a sixteenth share in Covent Garden Theatre, for which he composed much music. Some years later, after the death of his first wife, he travelled through Russia and Germany, eventually reaching Vienna, where he met and married Anna Selina Storace, first Susanna in *The Marriage of Figaro*. But this unfortunate marriage and their respective careers subsequent to it have nothing to do with Ranelagh, 1775.

Among the vocal performers was our friend Vernon, the tenor, and also Reinhold, the bass. This was presumably Reinhold the Younger, (1737 – 1815), son of one of Handel's bass singers of German origin. He was on the pay-roll of Covent Garden, and was also well known at the Pleasure Gardens, especially Marylebone, where, besides singing the usual type of ballads, he gave imitations ' of the Italian, German and French Stile of Singing,' somewhat after the fashion of Charles Bannister.

There was, of course, a Regatta Song, of which four verses will probably suffice :

Ye lords, and ye ladies, who form this glad throng,
Be silent a moment, attend to my song ;
And while you suspend your fantastical round,
Come bless your sweet stars that you're none of you drown'd.
    Derry down, down ; derry down !

. . . . . .

For say, should Britannia, ungratefully treat
The friend of her commerce, the nurse of her fleet ?
Shall he who with toil wafts your treasures to shore
In her hours of amusement be thought of no more ?
    Derry down, down ; derry down !

Array'd in his best, in his holiday clothes,
To-night the gay Thames his assistance bestows ;
And as usual to render the show more compleat
We have ransack'd the wardrobe of Tavistock Street.
　　Derry down, down ; derry down !

　　　　　. . . . . .

We've strove to amuse you by water and land,
Once Torre*, to please ye, had fire at command ;
To charm ye should be all the elements care,
So next time we'll fix on a plan in the air.
　　Derry down, down ; derry down !

The promise made in jest in the last couplet was fulfilled many years later in earnest, as will be seen hereafter.

Ranelagh Gardens, meant for light-hearted amusement, were the scene of a tragedy in the season of 1775. Sir Thomas Robinson had installed as housekeeper in Ranelagh House an old school and college friend who had fallen on evil days. He and his wife had free lodging, coals and candles, with a salary of £150 per annum, and seemed comfortably established, but one night the unfortunate gentleman got up and threw himself into the Canal. William Hickey was studying perspective and geometry with Mr. Malton, who lived exactly opposite the avenue leading up to Ranelagh, and had been presented by this same housekeeper with a silver ticket of admission, which allowed him not only to attend the evening entertainments, but to spend his mornings roaming about the Gardens, rowing on the canal, or playing tunes on the harpsichord in the Rotunda. The suicide of this friend was a grievous shock to the Malton family, and to William Hickey himself.

---

* Torre was a famous 18th-century pyrotechnist.

V

1776 – 1783

WAR WITH AMERICA AND FRANCE

(THE WAR OF AMERICAN INDEPENDENCE)

THE year after the Regatta saw the beginning of a decline both in Ranelagh's fashion and in the quality of its music, from which it made a brilliant recovery about 1790. Meanwhile, there were complaints that the management did not pay the members of the orchestra enough 'to appear decent,' so that they lost the best players, and in their stead was 'a set of mere scrapers,' many of whom were fit only to perform at puppet-shows. The management replied that, as the promenaders did not listen to the music anyway, it would be a waste of money to have expensive performers. The writer of a letter to the *Morning Post* retorted that it would be better to have no music at all, for bad music was only an interruption to conversation.

Refreshments often ran out before the evening was over, although late-comers' money was unscrupulously taken at the doors, and the lights would be extinguished for the sake of economy before two-thirds of the company were gone. The

' clumsy ale-house benches,' which had been placed round the fireplace in 1775, came in for censure, and it was suggested that the heavy iron chandeliers which hung from the ' rotten roof ' were a danger.

But worse than all this was the practice of opening the premises to the public out of the proper season, and without the usual entertainments. Soon Ranelagh would become ' notorious for private assignations ; its retired situation renders it extremely convenient for the purpose, and being left in the care of a housekeeper entirely, she, if viciously inclined, may not only accomodate the visitors, but even make her own daughters, if she has any, the principal actresses.'

The waiters, too, were getting out of hand. Not only did they ask for gratuities, but they insulted the company when refused. This was worse than the revolt of the American Colonies. What was the world coming to ?

* * *

The trial for bigamy of Elizabeth Chudleigh, alias the Duchess of Kingston, alias the Countess of Bristol, in Westminster Hall was a formidable counter-attraction that April, and distracted the people's thoughts even from America. Walpole wrote to Sir Horace Mann on April 17th : ' You may think of America, if you please, but we think and talk of one subject, the solemn comedy that is acting in Westminster Hall.' In September, 1773, the Duke of Kingston had died, leaving Elizabeth his estate for her life, on condition she did not remarry. She travelled extensively in Italy for a while, as usual attracting much attention ; the Romans were impressed by her yacht sailing up the Tiber, and she received marks of favour from Clement XIV. During her absence, Evelyn Meadows, the Duke's nephew, caused a bill of indictment for bigamy to be drawn up against her, acting on information he had obtained from Ann Cradock, the confidential maid. A short while before the opening of the case, Augustus Hervey's brother at last died, making him Earl of Bristol.

The trial was ' a sight which for beauty and magnificence exceeded anything' except a coronation, although the lady now had few vestiges of that beauty that was once so famous. ' Iphigenia ' was now large and ill-shaped, and looked like ' a bale of black bombazeen.' The nobility and gentry enjoyed a trial of this kind as much as they did a masquerade or a regatta. Those in the Duke of Newcastle's party at the opening were lucky, for ' a fine cold collation of all sorts of meats and wine, with tea &c ' was provided for his friends.

After a trial lasting five days, she was pronounced guilty, but escaped being burnt in the hand by claiming the privilege of her peerage. (She was undoubtedly Countess of Bristol, though not Duchess of Kingston.) She then left England for Calais in an open boat, and subsequently led a varied life of travel and scandal, but she was seen in the Rotunda no more, and her name soon fell out of conversation. She died in Paris in 1788.

*   *   *

In May of 1776 the town was ' running mad ' to see Garrick's last appearance. This indeed was the end of an epoch. Duchesses and Countesses cheerfully crowded into the Upper Boxes, the worst places in the house, merely to see him. His curse at the end of the first Act of *King Lear*, and his appeal to heaven at the end of the second, caused ' a kind of momentary petrefaction through the house, which he soon resolved as universally into tears,' and it took Sir Joshua Reynolds three days to recover from these emotions. His actual farewell on June 10th was ' too distressing to be described.'

Scarce had that excitement died down than there was the execution for forgery of Dr. Dodd, on June 27th, to keep society from feeling bored. Dr. Dodd had been a popular preacher, an active promoter of charity and was well known in every rank of London life. Appeals against the sentence were signed by many persons of wealth and position, and sympathy was almost universal. Streets on the way to Tyburn were crowded with the curious or the sympathetic on the day of the execution.

A Loyalist family from Richmond, Virginia, entered London through Newgate Street that day – after a voyage which had been varied by one shipwreck and one sea-fight – and beheld ' a countless throng, every hat was off, the windows were crowded.' When they learnt the cause, ' how deep was the effect upon their sympathies,' and ' with awe and sadness ' their coach was ' turned into another street, by which they reached their destination.'

It was the practice at taverns such as the Bedford or the Rainbow (where Ranelagh tickets could usually be obtained) to make up parties to attend the next day's hangings. Among the frequenters of the Shakespeare who went to see Dr. Dodd die at Tyburn was the composer Abel. But his good friend J. C. Bach, although he considered it right that Dr. Dodd should pay the penalty for his crime, stayed at home ; he said he could not admire anyone who would take the front seat in the Tyburn boxes to see a human being die like a dog in a string.

* * *

But in spite of these counter-attractions, and in spite of all the criticisms levelled at it, Ranelagh was still frequented by the *ton*, and some remarkable fashions were exhibited in the Rotunda. The macaronis wore enormous cut steel buttons on their short coats, and enormous silver or filigree buckles on their red-heeled shoes ; on their heads were pyramids of curls, and the tall canes they carried were sometimes swathed with green and silver binding. Ladies' headdresses were rising higher and higher ; before a party it took a skilled hairdresser three hours to complete one of these erections, which would not be demolished and re-erected until the next important occasion made it necessary. If in the meanwhile, the lady could not sleep in comfort, or if her hair should become rather smelly, or even if mice should nest in it, those were minor details. Fashion must be followed.

Ranelagh's singers this year included Mrs. Smith, Mrs. Bayntoun and Mr. Meredith – none of them stars of the first magnitude. Mrs. Smith was singing at Drury Lane that season, and left Ranelagh in the course of the summer to go to Liverpool with a company of singers. She was sufficiently well-known for a song from *The Deserter* to be included in one of Corri's volumes as ' sung by Mrs. Smith.' Mrs. Bayntoun and Mr. Meredith were ' good middling singers.' Meredith may have been some relation to the Liverpool bass of the same name, who was well known as an oratorio singer at the end of the century and beginning of the next. One night the Smith-Bayntoun-Meredith trio sang *A Bacchanalian Triumph*, with words by Mr. Bate and music by Theodore Smith.

In July the promenaders were shocked by the news of rioters at Shepton Mallet setting out to destroy some spinning jennies and being fired on by the Military. But although disquieting news came daily from America, it was not until August 10th that they knew that ' the Congress resolved upon independence on the fourth of July ; and it is said, have declared war against Great Britain in form.' There was great difficulty in enlisting men for the American War, so bad were conditions in both the services. Eight hundred sailors were ' pressed ' in London alone in 1776, and a large number of convicts who could no longer be transported to the colonies were passed into the army and navy.

Early that year had been published the first part of Mr. Gibbon's *Decline and Fall of the Roman Empire*. There were those who saw some parallel between the last days of the Roman empire and the strange times through which they themselves were passing. Horace Walpole decided at the end of June that, whatever happened in America, this country was undone.

* * *

Ranelagh's regular programme on Mondays, Wednesdays and Fridays (exclusive of special balls, gala concerts, masquerades, etc.) consisted in ' the usual vocal and instrumental concerts ' ; the time-table was ' horns and clarinets at seven, and the band at half past seven,' with horns and clarinets ' between the acts,' and the usual tea and coffee, for which the inclusive charge was 2s. 6d. Ladies and gentlemen were admitted ' to walk in the Rotunda and Gardens ' every day except Sunday for 1s. Let us hope that this privilege was not abused in the way suggested by the critics of the previous year.

The fashionable world kept very late hours. Horace Walpole said the American War had failed to bring people to their senses. ' Silly dissipation rather increases, and without an object. The present folly is late hours. Everybody tries to be particular by being too late, and as everybody tries it, nobody is so. It is the fashion now to go to Ranelagh two hours after it is over. The music ends at 10 ; the company go at 12.' Mr. Burke's pamphlet on the American War, and Mr. Sheridan's new comedy, *The School for Scandal*, gave people something to talk about early in May when they walked in the Gardens or the Rotunda, while dark clouds hung over the east and west. Fighting continued with varying success in America.

Lord Chatham appeared in the House of Lords on May 30th and made an appeal to the King to put an end to hostilities in America by putting an end to grievances. He was in favour of giving the Americans all they asked except their independence. The Dukes of Grafton and Manchester, Lord Camden and the Bishop of Peterborough, supported him, but the motion was rejected by a majority of 99 to 28.

*   *   *

Ranelagh lost its Maypole and Garden of Delights, Sir Thomas Robinson, on March 3rd, 1777. He had been an able director of its entertainments as well as profuse in private hospitality, and was one of the most picturesque figures of his time. His tall, thin form was often clad in hunting dress, with light green jacket, postilion's cap, and buckskin breeches. It is hardly surprising that when he went to Paris in this attire he was asked by an astonished Abbé if he were ' the famous Robinson Crusoe, so remarkable in history.' He had built himself a house, Prospect House, opposite Ranelagh House, and this house, ' with a most extensive and pleasing view of the Surry and Kentish hills, and river Thames,' was taken for the 1778 season by one Lee, who laid in an assortment of choice wines and advertised *petits soupers* at what he called the Ranelagh Subscription House. Ranelagh repudiated the connection in the press, and said it had no concern in the Subscription House advertised by Mr. Lee. In a letter to the *Town and Country Magazine* signed 'Ambulator,' there were dark hints about Mr. Lee's establishment. ' This latter place is at present supported by subscription, but does not fill so fast as was expected. The *petits soupers* create suspicions ; old husbands do not like that young wives should be wrecked upon a *Lee-shore*, though probably it may be as safe a navigation as any upon the banks of the Thames.'

Ranelagh proper (as opposed to Ranelagh improper) went on much as before, in spite of the death of its Maypole and Garden of Delights. In February (while France was concluding an alliance with the American States) the Treasurer invited any ' persons willing to serve the undertaking by contract ' with various necessary articles to submit their estimates to him at Ranelagh House by the 28th of the month. The articles in question were : ' The best hyson, or green tea ; the best Turkey coffee, roasted fresh every day ; the best Epping butter and milk ; finest loaf sugar, and the fine rolls used at Ranelagh, and for washing the table linen ; the best spermacetti or chamber oil for lighting the lamps in the Rotunda and also for lighting the lamps upon the road leading to, and within the Gardens of the Rotunda, either with or without the lamp irons.'

The Gardens opened in April, and it was expressly stated that there would be good fires in the Rotunda, passages and rooms adjoining. During that April, war with France was hourly expected, and on May 11th William Pitt the Elder, Lord Chatham, died. Even Horace Walpole admitted that, with all his defects, he would be ' a capital historic figure,' but he did not go to the State Funeral. ' You cannot conquer America,' Lord Chatham had said at a time when the war seemed to be going in our favour. ' If I were an American as I am an Englishman, while a foreign troop was landed in my country, I never would lay down my arms – never, never, never ! '

It was during this time of uncertainty and foreboding that Horace Walpole went to a fashionable party after the opera, and recorded that ' Lady Melbourne, who was standing before the fire, and adjusting her feathers in the glass, remarked " Lord ! they say the stocks will blow up ! That will be very comical " ' The nobility and gentry began to feel the depression. Fine houses were being sold for a mere song, and there was a marked diminution in the number of coaches and carriages on roads.

But it was a halcyon summer, and Ranelagh still had its patrons on warm evenings. Mr. Meredith was again ' a vocal

performer,' and Mrs. Farrell sang the praises of her ' Yellow
Hair'd Laddie ' to the strains of James Hook.

*   *   *

The winter of 1778-79 had been a hard one, and when the
Ranelagh season of 1779 opened it was promised that fires
would be kept up in the Rotunda ' while necessary.' Music was
heard on Mondays, Wednesdays and Fridays as before. The
Gentleman's Magazine reproduced the words of a song called
' The Court of Vauxhall,' which our friend Mr. Vernon sang
at that place of entertainment. It contained one verse deriding
the attractions of Vauxhall's rival, Ranelagh, which, we are
assured, was omitted in performance :–

> *The Lords and the Ladies who Ranelagh fill*
> *And move round and round like a horse in a mill*
> *Come hither al fresco to take a cool walk*
> *When tir'd of small coffee, small tea, and small talk.*

This merely echoed what many people were saying. In other
words, Ranelagh was becoming a bore. But the Lords and the
Ladies continued to fill it.

Dr. Arne died that March, surviving his contemporary and
only considerable rival, Dr. Boyce, by a year. Two months
before Dr. Arne's death, David Garrick – with whom he had
fought so many paper battles, and who was such a familiar
Ranelagh figure – had passed away. Chatham, Arne and Garrick, three of the greatest figures of the century in their different
spheres, left the scene in one of the worst years of its history.

On June 16th the Spanish Ambassador presented to the
British Court what was equivalent to a declaration of war.
Thirteen colonies were in revolt, we were at war with France
and Spain, there were threats of rebellion in Ireland, and we
were without a single ally. When the King closed the Parliamentary session on July 3rd, he said he esteemed it a happy

omen of the success of his arms that as difficulties increased, so increased the courage and constancy of his people. This was poor consolation to those who believed we were fighting a senseless and unrighteous war, but doubtless stimulating to those who believed the damned Americans, the damned Frenchies and the damned Dons deserved a good hiding and would get it.

In August the combined fleets of France and Spain appeared in the English Channel without opposition, and invasion was hourly expected. Mrs. Harris wrote to her son at St. Petersburg on the 22nd : ' We have an additional prayer in the Churches : that is all we have to avail us . . . ' A Royal Proclamation commanded all the horses and cattle to be driven inland from the coasts in the event of invasion. But the fleets withdrew early in September, and the immediate danger was over.

* * *

Whitehead, the Poet Laureate, poured contempt on France's naval pretensions in an Ode for the New Year 1780, which was set to music by Mr. Stanley :

> *And dares insulting France pretend*
> *To grasp the trident of the main*
> *And hope the astonish'd world should bend*
> *To the mock pageantry assum'd in vain?*

The relief of Gibraltar and the victory of Rodney in the West Indies that year indeed showed that Britannia was not going to relinquish the trident of the main to insulting France, Spain, Holland, America or any other country. Nevertheless, the years 1780-83 were years of danger and some humiliation for this country. As if war with France, Spain, Holland and America were not enough, June, 1780, brought the anti-Catholic Gordon riots, when London for four days was in the hands of the mob. People watched from their rooftops the fires raging, as they were to watch them in the winter of 1940-41. ' Confusion was trumps,' as Walpole said. But order was restored at last, after much damage to property, and Lord George Gordon was arrested at his house in Welbeck Street on June 9th. Lord North's government was increasingly (and deservedly) unpopular ; his resignation, when it came in 1782, was a defeat for the King himself. That defeat was final and it meant the end of any attempt at personal rule by a sovereign in this country. Leadership was restored to Parliament and to parliamentary leaders, and in 1783 William Pitt the younger, not yet twenty-five years old, became Prime Minister, and a new era opened. Meanwhile, the disastrous year of 1781 saw the virtual termination of the American War, to be followed at the end of 1782 by a somewhat humiliating peace. In India, Warren Hastings was saving British dominion by methods which were afterwards to be questioned. It was a confused pattern, the meaning of which only became plain many years afterwards.

*   *   *

During those perilous uneasy years which preceded the peace and Pitt's accession to power, Ranelagh kept up its concerts and its masquerades, its tea and coffee drinking. Round and round the Rotunda, or up and down the Garden walks, moved the polite world, talking of politics and of war, certainly, but also of the fashions, of scandal, of love, of the theatre and of music. The Duke of Gloucester and his beautiful Duchess, with her three daughters by her first husband, the Ladies Waldegrave, showed themselves one evening to the company at Ranelagh, soon after the Gordon riots had died down, when the rioters, most of them ex-convicts, were being tried. There was a ' thirty sixth share ' to be disposed of that year by Mr. Stirling, Attorney-at-law in Northumberland

Street, but there is no record as to who purchased this investment.

And it was in that black summer of 1780 that Miss Morris sought to distract attention from the serious state of affairs by singing Michael Arne's rondo, *Invitation to Ranelagh* :–

> *Hither Nymphs and Swains repair*
> *Quit the baleful scenes of strife*
> *Leave the rugged paths of care*
> *And taste of joys that sweeten life.*

Miss Morris, one of the lesser ' singing-actresses ' of the period appeared the next season also, together with Mrs. Barthelemon and Mlle Gavos. The last-named lady sang for the first time, and is described as possessing ' all the essentials of a good singer, but evidently wants tutoring.' Of Mrs. Barthelemon it is unnecessary to say more ; she certainly wanted no tutoring.

Nymphs and swains wore simpler fashions this season. The towering headdresses had practically disappeared, and ladies' hair was puffed out from the face, with curls falling on the shoulders. Hats were large and trimmed with ribbons or great ostrich plumes. Hoops had disappeared, but skirts were still full, and were held out by pads on the hips. Soft fichus were worn on the shoulders, and ruches of muslin or lace were a favourite trimming. A kind of riding-dress with a jacket of masculine cut was found to be becoming. (It was a forerunner of the tailor-made.) Fanny Burney saw ladies at a ball at Tunbridge Wells in the 80's who would have made 'admirable men.' The war was partly responsible for this fashion. ' Camber ' wrote to the *Gentleman's Magazine* in 1781 that he had ' long been very sensible of the several improvements which the military spirit, so prevalent in these kingdoms, and the several incampments, have introduced into the most distant counties,' but goes on to describe the deleterious effect of a visit to the camp at Coxheath upon the costume, and (by inference) the morals, of some young ladies ' in the inland part of England.' He arrived ' in the dog days,' and finding the young ladies sitting in an alcove in their riding-habits instead of their cool chintzes, expressed a fear that he had prevented them from taking their morning ride. They assured him they did not mean to stir out. One of them went to fetch ' her work,' clapping on ' a vast hat with a cockade ' as she left the room, and showing the horrified ' Camber ' that the back of her hair was ' clubbed.' ' Female delicacy is changed into masculine courage, and as much of the garb assumed as at first view almost leaves the difference of sex undistinguishable.' Gentlemen's attire was also simpler. The macaroni had disappeared, and the dandy had not yet arrived on the scene.

That season, 1781, some ' modern instrumental music ' was introduced, ' which blended with the heavy grandeur of the ancients ' promised an entertainment ' more adapted to the present taste than what has hitherto been given.' Something will be said later of these programmes of contemporary music. Evidently there was an attempt to raise the standard. May was chilly, and ' good fires are and will be kept while necessary.' Ladies and gentlemen could still walk in the Rotundo (sic) and Gardens for one shilling ; the concerts were as usual on Mondays, Wednesdays and Fridays. Tickets could be obtained at Ranelagh House itself, or at the Marine Society's Office, the London Tavern or the Jamaica, New Lloyds, Old Lloyds, the Rainbow, Batson's, London and Grays Inn Coffee Houses, at the Free Mason's Tavern in Great Queen Street, and at the famous Cocoa Tree in Pall Mall and the Thatched House in St. James's.

' Cargoes of bad news ' continued to arrive from east and west, and as if the scourges of war were not terrible enough, Jamaica had recently been swept by a terrible hurricane. Parliament voted £120,000 for the relief of sufferers on January

25th, and on May 3rd Ranelagh gave a concert of vocal and instrumental music 'for the BENEFIT of the Unhappy SUFFERERS in the late dreadful Hurricanes in JAMAICA and the BARBADOES.'

One of the most talked of pictures in the Royal Academy that summer was Sir Joshua's group of the three Ladies Waldegrave, Horace Walpole's great-nieces, who had been so much admired at Ranelagh the year before. Mr. Gainsborough also had some fine pieces on exhibition.

*   *   *

When Ranelagh opened on April 3rd, 1782, the promenaders doubtless talked over the new ministry of Rockingham, which had succeeded the fall of Lord North. Rockingham's task could not have been easy in any circumstances. An end had to be put to the American War by some means or other, and Irish grievances had to be satisfied. On April 16th, a fortnight after Ranelagh's opening, Mr. Grattan moved in the Irish Commons for a ' Declaration of Rights,' in the form of an Address to the Throne. It was passed unanimously by both Houses, and Rockingham's ministry was forced to grant the Irish nominal legislative independence. But the problem was shelved, not solved. The Irish Parliament was dominated by an Executive appointed from England. The Irish Catholics were still held down by their Protestant rulers, and discontent smouldered. The Cabinet, composed of five Rockingham and five Shelburne Whigs with the Tory Chancellor Thurlow, was doomed from the outset because William Pitt refused either to serve in it or to support it. It was a season of anxiety and bad news, tempered only by the glorious victory of Admiral Rodney in the West Indies, but London society continued to amuse itself. Horace Walpole thought our insensibility came from our being so dissipated, and also so accustomed to bad news.

Pastor Moritz, who visited Ranelagh that summer, was indeed disappointed when he had paid his half-crown and entered by the Garden door to find so few lights and so few people in the Gardens, and was faintly shocked when he was accosted by a young lady who asked him why he was walking thus solitarily. But his first view of the Rotunda made him think of the fairy tales he had read as a child. The lights, the organ, the vocal and instrumental music, even the refreshments, struck him as surpassing everything of the kind he had seen before. (Mr. Hudson was among the singers to be heard that year, and in his repertoire was ' Content, A Pastoral from Cunningham's Collection, set by Mr. W. Goodwin.') ' All around, under this gallery, are handsome painted boxes for those who wish to take refreshments : the floor is covered with mats, in the middle of which are four high black pillars ; within which there are neat fire-places for preparing tea, coffee and punch ; and all around, also, there are placed tables, set out with all kinds of refreshments. Within these four pillars, in a kind of magic rotundo, all the beau-monde of London move perpetually round and round.'

The Ambulator, or the Stranger's Companion in a Tour Round London of the year 1782 gives a more detailed account of Ranelagh both inside and out, part of which is worth quoting as showing the aspect of the Rotunda and Gardens at that period; and in what respect they had changed in the sixty years since their opening.

Upon entering the Rotunda, ' the first and principal object that strikes the spectator is, what was formerly the grand orchestra, but is now called the fire-place, erected in the middle of the rotundo, reaching to the cieling, and at the same time supporting the roof ; but it being found too high to yield to the company the full entertainment of the music, the performers were removed into another orchestra, erected in the space of one of the porticos : the former, however, still remains, an illustrious monument of the ingenuity of the artist, and is the most magnificent embellishment in the rotundo. It is a grand, beautiful, regular and complete structure, without the least dissonance or incongruity in any of its parts. It appears at first sight like a large and splendid column curiously and finely ornamented with paintings, carvings and niches.

' The circular pile is formed by eight triumphal arches of the Doric order. The pillars are divided into two stories : the first are painted in the resemblance of marble, and decorated with masks, and other ornaments ; and at the front of the arches are sconces on each side ; over these pillars are eight flower-branches of small lamps. The pillars in the second story are fluted and gilt, and surmounted with termini of plaister of Paris. Above the eight triumphal arches was the orchestra, which is now closed up, and several musical instruments are painted round it, being emblematic of its original design : the eight compartments which are made by the termini, and were formerly open, are decorated with festoons of flowers finely painted, resembling niches with vases and statues in them. The pillars which form the eight triumphal arches are the principal support of the grand and curious roof, which for size and manner of construction is not to be equalled in Europe : the astonishing genius of the architect is here concealed from our view by the cieling (sic) ; but it may easily be conceived, that such a roof could not be made and supported by any of the ordinary methods ; and if the timber-works above were laid open to public view, they would strike every beholder with amazement and admiration.

' The space on which this structure stands, is enclosed by a balustrade ; and in the centre is one of the most curious and admirable contrivances that ever the judgment of man could frame : it consists of an elegant fire-place that cannot smoak or become offensive. In cold weather it renders the whole rotundo very warm and comfortable. The chimney has four faces, and by tins over each of them, which are taken off and put on at pleasure, the heat is either confined or permitted to exhale, as it is found most agreeable to the company ; but the chief merit consists in having surmounted the many difficulties, and almost impossibilities, in erecting and fixing this fire place, which every architect on the slightest examination will instantly perceive . . . The chimney which proceeds to the top of the rotundo is of brick.

' . . . Round the rotundo are fifty two boxes for the accomodation of the company, with a table and cloth spread in each. In these the company are regaled, without any further expence, with tea or coffee. In each of these boxes is a droll painting, in the mimic masquerade or pantomime taste, and between each box hangs a bell-lamp with two candles in it . . . Before these paintings were put up, the backs were all blinds, that could be taken down and put up at pleasure ; but apprehensions arising that many people might catch cold by others indiscreetly moving them at improper times, it was resolved to put up paintings, and to fix them. These paintings were made for blinds to the windows at the time of the famous masquerades : the figures at that distance looked very well, and seemed to be the size of real life ; but now, being brought too near our view, they look rather preposterous. At the back of each box is a pair of folding doors, which open into the gardens . . . Each of these boxes will commodiously hold seven or eight persons.

' Over the boxes is a gallery fronted with a balustrade and pillars painted in the resemblance of marble, which contains the like number of boxes, with a lamp in the front of each ; and at the back is a blind that can be put up or taken down at pleasure, in order to render the boxes either airy or close, as is most agreeable to the company, and a pair of folding doors at the back of each, in the same manner as the lower ones.

' At the distance of ten boxes from the orchestra on the right hand is the King's box . . .

' The surface of the floor is plaister of Paris, over which is a mat, to prevent the company catching cold by walking upon it ; for this amusement of walking round the rotundo may be considered as one of the pleasures of the place . . . This mat answers another very useful purpose for, if the company were to walk on boards, the noise made by their heels would be so great, that it would be impossible to hear anything else ; but, the mat, being soft, not a step is perceived, and thus the music is heard in every part of the rotundo, and conversation is not interrupted by a disagreeable clangor. However, for the sake of balls, which are occasionally given here when the entertainments are over, two spaces are left unmatted from two of the porticos opposite each other to the fire-place in the centre. Formerly there were two sets of company dancing almost every night, who continued as long as they thought proper, and each was provided with a band of music from the orchestra.

' The cieling is painted a kind of olive colour, and round the extremity is a rainbow. From the cieling descend twenty chandeliers in two circles ; each chandelier is ornamented with a gilt crown, and the candles are contained in thirteen bell lamps, by which means they cast a more brilliant light . . . all parts shine with a resplendency, as if formed of the very substance of light ; then doth the masterly disposition of the architect, the proportion of the parts, and the harmonious distinction of the several pieces, appear to the greatest advantage, the most minute part by this effulgence lying open to the inspection.

' . . . The rotundo stands on higher ground than the Gardens ; it is surrounded on the back part by a gravel walk, which is lighted with lamps, and at the extremity of the eminence are planted shrubs and bushes. Here is a flight of steps, which descend to a beautiful octagon grass plat that is bounded by a gravel-walk, and shaded by elm and yewtrees. Contiguous to this beautiful spot are several little serpentine walks : in the evening they are lighted with lamps, which glitter through the trees, and have a pleasing effect.

' But the grand, and by some esteemed the finest, walk in the whole Gardens, is at the extremity on the left hand leading from the matted avenue, or covered way, at the south end of Ranelagh-house to the bottom of the gardens. This gravel walk is decorated on each side by a grass plat shaded with yew and elm trees, and lighted with twenty lamps, projecting from the latter. On an eminence at the bottom is a circular temple dedicated to Pan . . .

' On the right side of the gardens is a beautiful canal, which in a warm evening diffuses an agreeable coolness, and renders the gardens still more pleasant.

' At the lower end of the canal is a grotto, below which is a pipe that communicates with the river Thames, for the use of carrying off the foul water in the canal and receiving fresh.

' On each side the canal are handsome gravel-walks, lighted with lamps and shaded with trees and hedges ; the latter of which are cut with the utmost exactness and look extremely neat. The walk on the left side of the canal is lighted with twelve lamps : but on the right side are two walks ; that next the water is lighted with ten lamps, and the other, which runs parallel with it, with thirty four ; this latter walk is a very fine and spacious one ; it is shaded on both sides with lofty trees, and from each is a pleasant prospect. On the right are the gardens of Chelsea hospital, and on the left the canal and Ranelagh gardens. At the bottom of the walk are twenty lamps set in three triumphal arches, which extend from one side of the walk to the other, and in the evening, make a most charming and beautiful appearance. Here we meet the walk . . . that comes from the water, and by which the company enter the gardens.'

' Ambulator ' explains that those who come by water land at

a convenient flight of steps and pass along a gravel walk, with a view of the south front of Chelsea Hospital to their left, and of the river and the fields of Battersea on the opposite shore to their right. Thus they enter the gardens just below the canal, and pass up one of the shady gravel walks to the house or the Rotunda. Those who come by land pay their half-crowns to ' the proper person attending at the front of Ranelagh house,' and then pass through the house into the gardens, unless the weather is bad, when they go direct to the Rotunda by the covered way which connects it with the house.

The gardens first seen by those arriving by carriage or on foot are the upper gardens, lying between the Rotunda and the house. They too are laid out in gravel-walks and grass-plats, shaded by trees. 'A delightful fragrance exhales from an inclosed spot near the centre, which has been converted into a flower garden,' ' Ambulator ' notes, and this is a reminder to us that gardens in the eighteenth century did not always contain flowers.

One more ' agreeable feature ' remains to be mentioned : ' To prevent any offensive admission of servants, either by mistake or favour, the proprietors have been at the expence of erecting an handsome and convenient amphitheatre, with good seats, for their reception only : it is situated in the most proper place, being in the coach way leading to Ranelagh house, and at such a distance, that the servants can answer the instant they are called, which prevents a good deal of trouble and confusion.'

Some did not find Ranelagh refreshments sufficient, and Mr. T. Scott, of the Gentlemen's Hotel, Pall Mall, ' at the earnest solicitations of many respectable persons who frequented the polite place, Ranelagh Gardens,' opened a house at ' great expence ' where they might retire for ' suppers and suitable refreshments, so necessary to give a relaxation to that fatigue which the constant walking in the Rotunda and gardens

VI

1783 – 1793

AGAIN BETWEEN TWO WARS

Pitt's Ministry, formed at the end of December, 1783, had a stormy passage in the early months of 1784, and in April he went to the country. The result was an overwhelming triumph for the Tories. Pitt was back in office with a large majority as Prime Minister and remained Prime Minister for another seventeen years.

Ranelagh's opening night, Easter Monday, came in the middle of the election campaign, and was thinly attended. Belles preferred electioneering jaunts to the promenade of fashion, ' the polling booths must close before Ranelagh opens,' and ' the gaiety of the place would not be restored ' until ' the race to the winning-post of St. Stephen's was over.'

All the thoughts and energies of the great Whig ladies were concentrated on the Westminster election, in support of Charles James Fox. Dressed in ' garter blue and buff ' (the colours of their party), the beautiful young Duchess of Devonshire and her sister Lady Duncannon went canvassing, while the Tories enlisted the Marchioness of Salisbury on their side.

The Prince of Wales took an active part in the Whig campaign, opposing his father's policy and his father's friends whenever possible. After his triumph, Fox was carried through the streets on a laurel-decorated chair, with the Prince of Wales's plume and a flag inscribed ' Sacred to Female Patriotism ' before him. Ladies in blue and buff formed part of the cortège ; the houses of sympathisers were illuminated and the windows of opponents broken. The Prince of Wales gave a fête on the lawn of Carlton House, in celebration. Never, indeed, was such election fever. Horace Walpole overheard a little girl saying : ' Mama and I cannot get Papa over to our side.'

When this excitement had died down, and Whigs and Tories had time to go to Ranelagh once more, they heard the band led by Mr. Napier ' with great spirit,' and some new-comers in the vocal department : Mr. & Mrs. Warrell and Mr. Wilson, as well as Mrs. Bottarelli (probably the wife of Bottarelli, librettist to the King's Theatre). The Warrell's (or Warrel's) were what was known as ' respectable performers ' ; their daughter, later Mrs. Atkins, was more distinguished as a singer, and had the advantage of being trained by Rauzzini. Mr. Wilson is described as a ' soprano,' which presumably meant a falsetto and not a castrato. The standard of singing at Ranelagh at this time was low compared with what it had been during the reign of Dr. Arne, but was to be raised within a year or two.

It was a bad time for music and the polite arts generally, considered Mr. Twining.[1] ' Many masters [*i.e.*, music-masters] once in great business, are now wholly scholarless, without any other cause assigned but the general declension of the kingdom.' Even Dr. Burney had suffered from the bankruptcies of schools.

Yet on May 26th there took place one of the great musical events of the century, the Handel Commemoration in Westminster Abbey, followed by another day's music in the

[1] *Recollections of a Country Clergyman.*

Pantheon. Ranelagh's music was small beer in comparison.
Upwards of five hundred professional musicians took part in
this festival, and Burney considered it was the greatest aggre-
gation of vocal and instrumental performers the world had
ever seen. George III and the Royal Family were warm sup-
porters of the Commemoration, which was repeated in 1785,
1786, 1787, and 1791. A large sum of money was thereby
raised for the Society of Musicians, even in that year of stress
and difficulty.

That September, ballooning began to be the fashion, and
although it was to be many years before Ranelagh advertised a
balloon ascension among its attractions, ' balloon hats ' were
worn that year in the Gardens. Montgolfier had made his first
ascent in Paris on August 27th, 1783, and on September 15th,
1784, Lunardi, the Secretary to the Italian Embassy, ascended
from the Artillery Ground in London, and descended at
Stondon near Ware. This appeared to Horace Walpole as
childish as the flying of kites by school-boys. The possibility of
aerial travel and aerial warfare did not appeal to him. He had
no desire to imagine ' how much more expeditiously the east,
west or south will be ravaged and butchered, than they have
been by the old-fashioned clumsy method of navigation.'
About this time Thomas Smart, organist of St. Clement
Danes, wrote music to a popular Pleasure Gardens song on
this topic, called the Air Balloon : —

> Tho' miracles cease, yet wonders increase,
>   Imposition plays up her old tune
> Our old Gallic neighbours' scientifical labours
>   Have invented the Air Balloon.
>
> Should war 'gain break out, as 'tis not a doubt
>   With some that it may happen soon,
> The French will invade us, their troops all parade us
>   Brought o'er in an Air Balloon.

Then ships will appear, not in water but air,
And come in a twinkling down
From Calais to Dover, how quick they'll be over
Blown up by the Air Balloon !

At the end of the year which saw Pitt's triumph, and the first balloon ascension from London, Dr. Samuel Johnson died.

*   *   *

Was it the new Ministry of Pitt that infused new life into Ranelagh as into the whole country ? At all events, the music took a distinct turn for the better in 1786 – 1785 having been more or less a repetition of 1784.

Mr. Napier still led the orchestra, and was assisted by two wood-wind players of eminence : Mr. Decamp, and Mr. Patria, who played concertos on the German flute and the oboe respectively.

Gregorio Patria came to London some time in the 1780's, presumably from Italy, and was ' an eminent hautbois player ' at the end of the century, but somewhat overshadowed by Fischer, Gainsborough's son-in-law.

Mr. Wilson, ' the first serious man,' appeared once more, and is said to have improved since last season. But the management evidently decided they must spend a little more money on the vocal side, and so they introduced to the 1786 audiences ' Miss Mahon,' who was engaged at a very considerable salary.

The Mahon's were one of the most remarkable musical clans of the eighteenth century. They resemble the Youngs both in talent and in the confusion which inevitably arises when so many members of the same family are engaged in the same profession. They seem to have come from Salisbury originally, and to have settled at Oxford, where ' Mr. Mahon ' and ' Mrs. Mahon ' (who sang) produced between 1750 – 1770 five daughters all gifted with exceptional voices – three at least of whom were eminent as professional singers – and two sons, William and John, who were the leading clarinet players of their generation. The daughters appeared as ' the Miss Mahons ' or as ' Miss Mahon and Miss M. Mahon,' and later under their respective married names : Mrs. Ambrose, Mrs. Warton, Mrs. Munday and Mrs. Second.

The young lady who made her debut in 1786 is described as a sister to the celebrated performer on the clarinet of that name, as having studied at Oxford, and possessing great vocal abilities, highly improved by a scientific education, as well as the irresistible attractions of ' a fine countenance and an elegant form.' All of this might have been said of any one of the Mahon daughters, but for various reasons it seems likely that this one was Sarah, the future Mrs. Second. (Mrs. Munday made her debut at Ranelagh a few years later, as will be seen.)

The Rotunda, too, had undergone several judicious alterations, which were considered no less convenient than ornamental. ' Formerly the company were perpetually annoyed by the snuffing of the candles ; this is now totally removed by the patent lamp, which has a most splendid and beautiful effect, and being placed above the eye, it is not offended by the extreme brilliancy of the light.'

Gentlemen were no longer wearing swords in the Rotunda, and their wide-skirted coats were giving place to long tails. Their hair was dressed in a little queue at the back, with two or three horizontal curls at each side, somewhat resembling a barrister's wig. The ladies' hair was worn curled loosely, and was still puffed out at the sides, giving a totally different outline from the erections of the 1770's or the close dressing of the earlier part of the century. Sometimes large mob caps were worn over these coiffures, or fur-edged hoods. Simply trimmed and broad-brimmed straw hats were fashionable out-of-doors.

*   *   *

It was about this time or earlier that Samuel Rogers began regularly to frequent Ranelagh. He has nothing to say of its music, but considers it ' a very pleasing place of amusement,' and stresses that, although fashionable, it was not ' exclusive ' ; it was open to anyone who could afford to pay 2s. 6d. for admission, and ' there persons of inferior rank mingled with the highest nobility of Britain.' The fashionable hour to arrive at that time was between nine and ten o'clock, and in the Rotunda ' All was so orderly and still, that you could hear the whishing sound of the ladies' trains as the immense Assembly walked round and round the room. If you chose, you might have tea, which was served up in the neatest equipage possible.' Marylebone Gardens had disappeared in 1776, but rivalry with Vauxhall was still keen. St. James's Street used to be crowded in the evenings ' with the carriages of the ladies and gentlemen who were walking in the Mall, the ladies with their heads in full dress, and the gentlemen carrying their hats under their arms. The Proprietors of Ranelagh and Vauxhall used to send decoy-ducks among them, that is, persons attired in the height of fashion, who every now and then would exclaim in a very audible tone " What charming weather for Ranelagh " or " for Vauxhall." '

*   *   *

After the great effort of 1786, music seems to have declined again. The season of 1787 was one of financial loss, and in 1788 the value of the shares had dropped to £900. Retrenchment had to be the order of the day, and the management decided to open the season without any vocal performers. (And this was at a time when Vauxhall had a particularly strong team of

The full programme was as follows :—

Act I

Overture Occasional	...	...	Handel
Fourth Concerto	...	...	Avison
Song	... ...	...	Miss Mahon
Concerto, French horn	...	...	Messrs. Leander

Coronation Anthem
God Save the King with a full chorus on the joyful
RESTORATION OF HIS MAJESTY'S HEALTH

Act II

Overture, Acis and Galatea, with the chorus O the Pleasures
of Plains

Concerto, clarinet	...	...	Mr. Mahon
Overture	... ...	...	Bach
Overture	... ...	...	Haydn
Concerto violin	...	...	Mr. Ashley, junior
Song	... ...	...	Miss Mahon

To conclude with God Save Great George our King in
full chorus

' O the Pleasures of the Plains ' and the Coronation Anthem
had been in Ranelagh programmes for many years, and were
specially popular during the reign of Dr. Arne, but the
inclusion of an overture by Haydn shows a desire to be up-to-
date. One is glad to see the name of Avison, who was a contemporary of Dr. Arne and Dr. Boyce, and had died in 1770.
He studied with Geminiani the violinist, singing-master of
Mrs. Arne, (Cecilia Young 1) wrote an *Essay on Musical
Expression*, and became organist in his native town, New-
castle-on-Tyne. There is no indication which of his fifty concertos was given on this occasion. One or two of them have
been republished and performed recently with success. We do
not know which ' Overture ' of Haydn's was performed, and

we are not even told the composers of the solo concertos, or of the songs. ' Bach ' to audiences of 1789 meant the English Bach, Johann Christian, the same who refused to go and see the execution of Dr. Dodd. After a busy life as opera and concert director, as well as music master in the Royal Family, he had died in 1782.

The orchestra on this occasion was decorated with ' a crown of variegated lamps,' with the letters G.R. on each side, and a scroll of coloured lamps spelling ' God Save the King.' We are glad to learn that this loyal demonstration was attended by a very respectable and select company, among whom were all the foreign Ambassadors, and many of the Nobility who continued in the vicinity of London during the holidays. (There would have been more had there not been a Ladies' Easter Ball at the Mansion House, a concert at the Haymarket, and other attractions on the same evening.) Most of the ladies were dressed in white, wearing white ribbons upon which ' God Save the King' or 'Long live the King' appeared in gold letters.

In the same issue of *The Times* which advertised this concert, the public were respectfully informed that the Exhibition and Sale of the late Mr. Gainsborough's Pictures and Drawings would open that day at his dwelling house in Pall Mall. (He had died the previous August.) They were respectfully informed that at Rice's Great Room (late Hickford's), Brewer Street, Golden Square, Mr. Kean would continue his Senatorial and Theatrical Imitations, in which he would be assisted by his brother Mr. E. Kean. As for international affairs, we read that the tumults in Paris were so great that no public business was going forward.

On May 19th Ranelagh held a second celebration of His Majesty's happy recovery, and engaged Mrs. Martyr, Miss Leary, Miss Poole (or Pool) Mr. Darley, and Mr. Incledon to sing, and Messrs. Hook, Pieltain and Parke to play.

Mrs. Martyr had only recently become Mrs. Martyr, and

had been already well known as Miss Thornton. She was of unusual charm and beauty : of middle height with a well-proportioned figure, with raven-black ringlets and black eyes which were renowned for the meaning glances they cast at her audiences, a retroussé nose, and a lovely complexion. Her voice was shrill and powerful, and she affected a staccato style of singing in imitation of Ann Catley – a singer of the previous generation who caused a sensation by her use of staccato and her charmingly impudent personality. Indeed, Mrs. Martyr seems to have deliberately modelled herself on Ann Catley, both in singing and acting, but she had more regular beauty than her predecessor and less natural gaminerie. Shield wrote a hunting bravura song, ' Old Towler,' to enable Mrs. Martyr to exploit her vocal mannerism. Neither Ann Catley nor her imitator was what would have been called a ' scientific singer.' But Mrs. Martyr made her debut as Rosetta in *Love in a Village*, and sang Louisa in *The Duenna*, Euphrosyne in *Comus*, and other lyric parts. In *The Follies of a Day* – a version of Beaumarchais' *Le Mariage de Figaro* by Thomas Holcroft, with music by Shield – she was an ideal Cherubino, ' ausserordentlich unschuldig verführerisch ' according to Brandes. Pasquin in *The Children of Thespis* compares her with Persephone and Cleopatra, to the detriment of those ladies, and writes as follows of her charms :–

> *See Harmony joyant burst wild on the stage*
> *To give a young sorceress up to the age*
> *'Tis all-alive MARTYR who claims Beauty's throne,*
> *And marks indirectly each gazer her own.*
>
> . . . . . .
>
> *Those rich sable locks which o'er shadow her brow,*
> *Frigidity warms, and provokes the fierce vow;*
> *In irregular ringlets they happily wave,*
> *To hook the blithe hearts of the wise, young and brave.*

In fact, Mrs. Martyr had every qualification for a popular Pleasure Gardens singer, and when she sang in the Rotunda, doubtless the blithe hearts of the wise, young and brave (as well, possibly, as those of the foolish, elderly and pusillanimous) were hooked in her irregular ringlets. She was a favourite singer of James Hook's songs at Vauxhall also, from 1786 – 1789.

Miss Leary, later Mrs. Franklin, was also one of Mr. Hook's young ladies. Her charms are not so much praised as those of Mrs. Martyr, but she must have been personable, she must have had the requisite humour and archness to sing such ballads as ' Never say no when you mean to say yes,' she must have had good articulation, and a reasonably flexible and agreeable voice, for she had a long innings at Vauxhall, singing there from 1786 to 1821. Both she and Mrs. Martyr were ' English ' singers, in the sense defined earlier in these pages.

Miss Poole, on the other hand, who was even better known later in her career as Mrs. Dickons, had been trained in *bel canto* by Rauzzini of Bath, and though much younger than Mrs. Barthelemon, she was capable of the same kind of ' Italian ' singing. She was a contemporary and rival of the Mahon sisters, and excelled in sacred music. (It was said that her ' Rejoice greatly ' and ' Let the bright Seraphim ' seldom failed to produce an encore.) Religion seemed to breathe from every note. *Jackson's Oxford Journal* of November 26th, 1785, tells us that ' On Thursday Night, the celebrated Miss Pool, not eleven Years of Age, performed two Songs, composed by Dr. Arne, at our Musick Room ; also played the twelfth Sonata of Paradies, which, making but a small allowance for her tender Years, has never been exceeded, if equalled, in this Century.' Her father placed her with Rauzzini at the early age of eleven says the *Georgian Era*, but this is probably an exaggeration. She was in her early teens when she sang at Vauxhall 1787 – 1790, and at Ranelagh in 1790. In the early 90's she

CHARLES INCLEDON

began to be well known at the Antient Concerts, the Covent Garden Oratorios and their like. In 1806 she married Mr. Dickons, and left the profession, but her husband had financial losses and she returned to singing. She was also a charming actress. In 1812 she sang Susanna in the first London production of *Figaro*, to the Countess of Catalani, and in 1818 Rosina in Bishop's adaptation of Rossini's *Barbiere di Seviglia*. She also sang with success in Italy. Ill-health compelled her to retire in 1822, and she died in 1833.

A portrait of Darley singing at Vauxhall shows a chubby, cheerful face with a cupid's bow mouth, beneath curly powdered hair, with a double chin nestling in a snowy stock, and a paunch which he is apparently propping up on the balustrade of the orchestra. Pasquin calls him ' a big suckling.' He was a popular robust singer of third or fourth rank at the Gardens and theatres, whom no one would have mentioned in the same breath as Incledon, Vernon or even Arrowsmith. Yet he sang their songs and played their parts when substitutes were required. Pasquin is unkind :–

> *When he tears, without Mercy, poor Music to rags,*
> *It resembles stern Boreas untying his bags*
>
> . . . . . .
>
> *But this minstrel would certainly add to our joys,*
> *Could the dolt be persuaded to chant with less noise.*

Charles Incledon was a singer of quite another calibre, indeed, one of the greatest tenors this country has ever known. Like Charles Dibdin and many another singer, he began his musical career as a choirboy soloist. He was born at St. Keverne, Cornwall in 1763 or 1758 (most probably in 1763), and baptised Benjamin, which name he afterwards discarded. His father, Bartholomew Incledon, was a surgeon. After about seven years at Exeter Cathedral, under Langdon and Jackson, Charles ran away to sea. When his voice broke and he lost the

P

privileges and prestige of an 'angel choirboy,' he probably chafed at Cathedral discipline, and like other restless adolescents hoped to find a freer and more adventurous life in the navy. More adventurous it certainly was, and he saw some active service, but the discipline was as strict as any imposed by a choirmaster. The privations and hardships suffered by those serving in His Majesty's navy at that time are sufficiently well known now, although the eighteenth-century public at large ignored them until they were brought home by the Spithead mutiny in 1797. Incledon must have been about fifteen when he sailed for the West Indies on board the *Formidable*, later changing to the *Raisonnable*, whose Captain was Lord Hervey, nephew of 'Iphigenia's' husband. Some years before, the name of Nelson appeared in the *Raisonnable's* books, and in 1801, when Incledon was at the height of his fame, she took part in the battle of Copenhagen. No account of his experiences survives, but we can be sure he lived hard. In after years the fact that he had been 'a real sailor' had considerable publicity value. His singing career coincided with a time of naval expansion, and his audiences appreciated the fact that when he sang 'Black Eyed Susan' or 'The Storm,' they were not listening to a mere landlubber.

The story goes that his voice and talents were noticed by the officers – perhaps, like Ralph Rackstraw, he sang in the rigging – and that gave him useful introductions to the managers at the end of his last voyage. His first appearance was with Collin's company at Southampton in 1784, as Alphonso in Arnold's *Castle of Andalusia*. The next year he was engaged at Bath, and he too had lessons with Rauzzini, the great master of *bel canto*. From 1786 to 1789 he had been singing regularly at Vauxhall in the summer months, but his debut in the London theatres was not until September 17th, 1790, when he appeared as Dermot in *The Poor Soldier* at Covent Garden.

When he helped Mrs. Martyr, Miss Leary, Miss Poole, and

Mr. Darley to celebrate His Majesty's happy recovery on May 19th, 1789, Charles Incledon was only at the beginning of what was to be a long and brilliant career. When he first appeared at Covent Garden in the following year, he found a public waiting for a first-class tenor. There was, indeed, no tenor with a voice of such quality and power at either of the Patent Houses. Michael Kelly was ' useful ' and experienced, no more. Charles Dignum's voice was not outstanding, though he filled many roles satisfactorily at Drury Lane. John Braham did not make his London debut until 1796, and then left England in 1797 ; Charles Incledon was without a rival until Braham's return in 1801. A taste for the pure tenor voice was growing, and castrato singing was on the wane. From 1790 until 1815 Incledon was loyal to Covent Garden, singing the usual repertoire of so-called English operas – *Artaxerxes*, *The Waterman*, *The Beggar's Opera*, *Love in a Village*, and so on. In the summer, he sang at the provincial theatres and at the Pleasure Gardens. In addition, he sang in subscription concerts and the oratorio, where his only rival was Samuel Harrison – an exquisite artist but with a voice that was renowned for its sweetness rather than its power. Incledon sang in Linley's Sacred Music Concerts, at John Ashley's Covent Garden Lenten oratorios, at the Oxford concerts, and in the first performance of *Creation* under John Ashley.

An article in the *Musical Quarterly* for 1818 speaks of his great natural endowments, and of his ' voice of uncommon power, both in the natural and falsetto . . . His natural voice was full, open, neither partaking of the reed nor the string, and sent forth without the slightest artifice ; and such was its ductibility that when he sung pianissimo it retained its original quality. His falsetto was rich, sweet and brilliant, but totally unlike the other. He took it about D, E or F, or ascending an octave, which was his most frequent custom. He could use it with facility, and execute ornaments of a certain class with

volubility and sweetness. His shake was good, and his intonation much more correct than is common with singers imperfectly educated. His pronunciation of words, however, was
coarse, thick and vulgar . . . He had a bold and manly way of
singing, mixed however with considerable feeling, that went
to the hearts of his countrymen . . . He sung like a true
Englishman . . . His forte . . . was ballad, and ballad not of the
modern cast of whining or wanton sentiment – but the original, manly, energetic strain of an earlier and better age of
English poesy and English song-writing, such as Black-eyed
Susan and The Storm.'

The chief criticism levelled at his singing was that he over-
used his beautiful falsetto. His studies with Rauzzini had not
been long enough to give him an extensive *bel canto* technique,
yet he had learnt enough to keep his voice fresh in spite of
constant public appearances, and he had acquired a certain
amount of ' Italian ' flexibility. We do not read that he ever
forced his voice, as Braham was apt to do. Nature seems to
have given him volume as well as quality, and he was wise
enough to leave well alone. Lee Lewes speaks of his ' strength
united with sweetness,' a rare union. An article in *The Gentleman's Magazine* (1815) emphasises the ' marvellous sweetness
and forcible simplicity of his style,' and Leslie probably meant
much the same when he said that his voice was ' the most
manly and at the same time the most agreeable ' he had ever
heard. ' Manliness ' was a quality which had begun to come
into fashion when the tenor voice first supplanted the castrato,
in John Beard's day, and it was particularly appreciated during
the years 1794 – 1815 when martial ardour swept the country.
Incledon's career coincided with the years of struggle with
France, and though he had forsaken the navy for a more lucra-
tive and less arduous profession, his patriotic sea-songs were
sung with conviction, and he had a bluff, nautical appearance
which was in keeping with the sentiments he sang. The

' sweetness ' of his voice enabled him to give effect to that pathos which was also becoming so fashionable. (The age of ' sensibility ' was beginning.) *The Musical Quarterly* speaks of him as ' imperfectly educated,' yet Crabb Robinson was impressed by his knowledge of Purcell and of Church music.

There is a story that he once sang ' The Storm ' to Mrs. Siddons in private. She wept, and taking hold of both his hands, said : ' All that my brother and I did is nothing compared with the effect you produce.' This effect was produced by vocal colour and dramatic singing alone, for as an actor he was no better (though probably no worse) than other tenors before and since. He good-humouredly admitted his own deficiencies, and said he was flattered when some ecclesiastical authority forbade his performance in a church on the grounds that he was an actor. ' You hear that,' he said to Jack Bannister, ' he calls me an actor ! ' Pasquin ends a panegyric on his singing with the lament

> *Could he act as he sings, what an object he'd be !*

and concludes philosophically that

> *. . . to meet with a VOCALIST fit to act well,*
> *Is a thought on which HOPE can scarce patiently dwell.*

Nor had he good looks or ' presence.' Leslie says he had the face and figure of ' a low sailor ' all his life. He was certainly portly, and had a taste for jewellery which scarcely suited his appearance. Crabb Robinson describes him as wearing seven rings on his fingers, five seals on his watch ribbon, and carrying a gold snuff box.

When John Braham came back from Italy in 1801 to sing at Drury Lane in English opera, Incledon had a younger rival with natural powers equal to his own. Each of the Patent Houses could flaunt a great tenor, as in the days of John Beard and Thomas Lowe. Each had his following. But they sometimes appeared together, as in *The Cabinet* (February 9th, 1802), and also *The English Fleet in* 1342 (December 13th, 1803), when their duet ' All's Well ' was unforgettable. In 1815 Incledon left Covent Garden and tried his fortunes in America, with small success as his powers were already waning. (He had been singing for over thirty years.) He died at Worcester in 1826, under seventy years of age.

Charles Incledon was the type of convivial artist of whom many stories are told, some of them doubtless apocryphal. He was one of that cheerful set which included Cooke, Henry Angelo, and Jack Bannister, and was not a teetotaller. Angelo tells us that to signify the line which separated sobriety from inebriety he would speak of crossing the Brook Kedron. His Cathedral training had given him an extensive acquaintance with the Scriptures and he was fond of profane jokes. He was married three times, and was not noted for conjugal fidelity. One of the ' Incledon stories ' concerns his confessions made to his wife when they were nearly shipwrecked on the way back from Ireland. At the height of the Napoleonic scare, he joined the Duke of Cumberland's Sharp Shooters, together with Cooke the tragedian, Bologna and Spencer, the harlequins and other players. On one occasion, the Duke was reviewing the corps at Chalk Farm, and a sham fight was in progress. The troops had to make their way over the Hampstead and Highgate Fields. The plump Incledon brought up the rear. ' My lad,' said he to a butcher boy, who was following the ' army ' after the manner of his kind, ' carry this damned gun for me, and I'll give you a shilling ! ' The urchin, delighted with the honour of carrying a real gun and the prospect of earning a shilling, gladly complied. The tenor, his equipment thus lightened, made better progress for a while, but was nearly thrown down because his sword kept getting between his legs. He spied a little girl among the onlookers. ' My little girl,' said he, ' do carry this damned sword for me, and I'll give you a

shilling!' The little girl did as she was requested, and at the halt
' Incledon made his appearance round and green as a cabbage,
accompanied by his male and female armour bearers, to the no
small amusement of the bystanders.' ' What a shame, that the
first singer in the world should be the last soldier in the field ! '
exclaimed Cooke.

*　　*　　*

The instrumentalists who performed at this celebration
concert on May 19th, 1789, were also of eminence in the
musical world, 'Mr. Pieltain' (Dieudonné Pascal) was born in
Liege in 1754, and was a pupil of Giornovichi. From 1778 –
1783 he played at the Concerts Spirituels in Paris, and in 1783
came to London, where he was first violin at the Hanover
Square, Professional and other concerts. In 1791 he became
conductor at Vauxhall, and two years later he went abroad.
He died in his native town in 1833. His brother was a celebrated horn-player in London at the same period, and married Miss Chenu, the singer. ' Mr. Parke ' was John Parke,
oboe player, born in 1745. In 1771 he succeeded Fischer as
concerto player at Vauxhall. He was chief oboe at the Lenten
oratorios in 1776, and soon after played solos at Ranelagh and
Marylebone. He was also in the King's Band, and in 1783
became Chamber Musician to the Prince of Wales. On this
occasion he is described as ' conductor,' which in eighteenth
century parlance meant the person in charge of the programme. The modern time-beating conductor did not exist in
those days, and the orchestra was kept together by the leader
of the violins and the continuo-player. He died in 1829. John
Parke's daughter, Maria Hester, sang at Ranelagh in 1792, as
will be seen hereafter. His brother, W. T. Parke (1762-1847),
also a renowned oboe player, composed many songs and concertos for Vauxhall, and the other Gardens, and was the
author of the readable but unreliable *Musical Memoirs*.

Later in the 1789 season, the Spanish Ambassador, the Marques del Campo, gave a gala at Ranelagh, also in celebration of His Majesty's happy recovery. The decorations ' far surpassed anything hitherto seen in that line.' Festoons of lamps adorned with artificial flowers were hung from the trees and round the canal. On the left-hand side of the canal there was a grand display of fireworks.

In the Rotunda, the Queen and the four Princesses listened to the music in a box covered in scarlet silk fringed with gold, and supped in another box hung with white silk. The orchestra was ornamented with natural flowers, and on one side of it was a stage – facing the Queen's box – upon which children danced Spanish dances, ' richly dressed.' Glees and catches were sung after supper from recesses on each side of the stage. There was space for the company to dance roped off by ropes covered in red baize. Those who wished to dance drew numbers from a wheel. But this did not interfere with the promenade, without which the Rotunda would not have been the Rotunda. The chandeliers were ornamented with natural flowers, and wax candles gleamed in baskets of flowers. The lower boxes in which the company supped were concealed by silk curtains striped blue and red, intended to depict ' a Spanish camp ' – each being guarded by a boy in Spanish uniform. When the curtains were drawn up, the supper tables were revealed, decorated alternately with baskets of flowers and ' temples.' The supper was served by one hundred *valets de chambre* dressed in scarlet, ' the seams adorned with broad gold lace, the coat lined with blue, with blue waistcoats bound with broad gold lace,' and one hundred footmen in sky blue coats and waistcoats, bound with silver. Damsels ' ornamented with wreaths of flowers ' made tea for the company. There were the choicest fruits and the most exquisite wines served, some of which had been sent from Spain for the occasion.

The impression left on the mind by reading a description of this scene is of something akin to a florid Italian aria sung by a *bel canto* singer, in which the melody is so embellished by ornaments and cadenzas as to be almost unrecognisable. There seems to have been scarcely a square inch of the Rotunda undecorated by flowers, coloured lights, gold tassels or silver braid.

The Queen and the Princesses with their retinue had come in twelve carriages, accompanied by a party of the Horse Guards, to Chelsea College, and had entered the Garden Gate on foot. The Duke of Gloucester and his son and daughter were also in the Royal party. The other Royal Dukes, as will be seen later, were at Ranelagh that evening, but not with their mother and sisters. When they first entered the Rotunda, there was an alarm of fire. The waxlights in the baskets of flowers suspended from the ceiling had been placed too near the flowers, which caught alight, but by ' great judgment and steadiness ' the fire was put out. It is one of the extraordinary features of Ranelagh's career that the Rotunda, though built largely of wood, survived for sixty-odd years and did not perish by fire, as did so many London theatres. (The Opera House was burnt down that same summer.)

The entertainment began with the singing of Colonel Arabin's Ode. The first verse will give a sufficient idea of the style of its poetry :–

> *Sweet, our sentiments impart*
> *Ev'ry throbbing breast rebounding*
> *Speak the feelings of the heart,*
> *Viewed by angels with delight*
> *Hark ! they shout, the King is living !*
> *Bend the knee and God adore !*

After the singing of this Ode came the Spanish dances, followed by God Save the King. Then the Royal party retired to extraordinary movement,' the French Revolution. But the opinions of the ladies and gentlemen who promenaded in the Rotunda were already divided on the subject. The more advanced Whigs agreed with Fox who greeted the news of the fall of the Bastille with ' How much the greatest event that has happened in the world, and how much the best ! ' Reformers and idealists looked forward to a new age. Reform Societies sent letters of congratulation to the French leaders. Even Pitt and the Tories rejoiced that France was now to have parliamentary government and a constitutional monarchy, those blessings which the Glorious Revolution of 1688 had conferred on this favoured isle, which had been fostered by Sir Robert Walpole during the years of peace, and which had survived even the policy of the King and Lord North during the black years preceding 1782. Pitt, too, believed friendship with France a guarantee of peace in Eastern Europe. But Burke already mistrusted the new movement. ' Whenever a separation is made between liberty and justice, neither is safe,' he wrote a few weeks after July 14th, 1789. And many others foresaw in the new principles a menace to their own privileges and to the divinely-established structure of society. Yet others, while approving the principles of the French reformers, saw much to deplore in their methods. Indeed, as the Ranelagh season wore on, it became plain that the French Revolution of 1789 was not at all like the English Revolution of 1688. But some – less concerned with principles – rejoiced at anything which promised to weaken the power of France, the hereditary enemy. Even Burke thought that she could now be considered as ' expunged out of the system of Europe.'

Meanwhile the trial of Warren Hastings dragged on, but was losing its drawing power. The public was tired of it, and sympathy with the accused was growing. Oratory had begun to pall. It was realised that Westminster Hall had been ' converted into a lyceum ; a school of eloquence ; and all was seen

confused and magnified through the mists of rhetorical decla-
mation.'

The Rotunda had opened on April 5th with a concert of
vocal and instrumental music. Miss Poole again sang, and Mr.
Griffiths was the male singer. One Ashley played a concerto on
the violoncello, and another Ashley on the violin. (The composers' names are not given.) The programme of orchestral
music includes concertos by Avison and Corelli, and overtures
by Handel, Haydn, Bach and Abel. Regular concerts of this
type continued throughout the season three times a week.

*   *   *

As a change, an Italian Serenata was performed on June
29th, ' by the desire of several persons of distinction,' consisting of favourite songs by Madame Mara, Signor Marchesi, and
other singers from the Italian Opera, and ' A variety of dancing ' by the dancers of that establishment.

Elizabeth Schmähling was born in Leipzig in 1749, and was
a violinist before she made her debut as a singer. She married
Mara, a 'cellist, from whom she soon separated. From 1784 to
1802 she made this country her chief home, and in opera,
oratorio and in concert arias she had no rival but Mrs. Billing-
ton. Her later years were unhappy. She was living on a
property she had bought at Moscow in 1812, and the French
invasion and the destruction of the city ruined her. Friends at
Reval supported her, and in 1819 she came back to London,
and gave a concert at the opera house with a view to raising
money. But the older generation could only mourn the decay
of her vocal powers, and a younger generation had arisen to
whom her glory was not even a memory. She died in Reval in
1833, at the age of 83. In that summer of 1790, Mme. Mara
was at the height of her fame – a *bel canto* singer of the old
school.

Signor Marchesi, too, belonged to the old school, and was

and a brilliant glory.') In spite of the variety of new and elegant costumes Messrs. Warder had offered the public, there
was ' a scarcity of good characters,' and most of the company
were in dominoes. There was, however, a variety of seasonable
viands, and abundance of good wine. His Royal Highness the
Prince of Wales honoured the celebration of his mother's
birthday from 2 a.m. to 5 a.m., with Lord Maynard in attendance. Their costume is not described.

*   *   *

In November Burke's *Reflections on the French Revolution*
appeared, the first attack of the counter-revolution. From then
onwards Burke preached a violent crusade against those he
considered the enemies of religion and civilisation. But Pitt
would not be moved. England would not depart from neutrality, unless self-defence made it necessary. Fox, on the other
hand, was a declared friend of the Revolution. Public opinion
was divided and muddled. This much was certain : everyone
was uneasy and no one wanted war. It was a time of industrial
development and economic prosperity throughout all England.
Men who were living in freedom and were making money were
naturally impatient of ideas and events which threatened what
was a satisfactory and comfortable way of life. Only the less
insular realised that conditions on the other side of the Channel were totally different. There were still young idealists like
William Wordsworth, who was on the Continent that year,
who saw the French experiment as the dawn of a wonderful
new age. Revolution Clubs flourished to a certain extent.
(There was a request that July 14th might be celebrated at
Ranelagh. This was refused, and flags and cockades sent from
France were stopped at the Customs.) Burke's *Reflections*
were answered by Paine's *Rights of Man*, a manifesto of the
extreme Radical and Republican school, which thoroughly
shocked and alarmed all but the extremists. A fairly common

mood was voiced by Mr. Twining when he wrote : ' I dread the meeting of Parliament – I dread war – I dread peace – I dread everything – the world cannot stand against these specious but false theories of government.'

Ranelagh gave a masquerade as early as February, 1791, under the patronage of the Prince of Wales and the Duke of York. Once again there is a complaint of the scarcity of ' characters.' Too many black dominoes gave a gloomy appearance. But an entertainment was provided by Lee Lewes and Wilson of Covent Garden in the characters of a mountebank doctor and his patient, and the supper provided by Mr. Daubigny was plentiful. A column in the press ends significantly : ' The wines were good. It was nine in the morning before the House was cleared.'

The real opening of Ranelagh was on Monday, April 25th, with a firework and a concert of vocal and instrumental music, in honour of the birthday of Princess Mary. Royal patronage was pulling up Ranelagh's popularity once more, and its fashion was now at its zenith.

Once yet again, ' by Desire and under the Patronage of His Royal Highness the Prince of Wales, Her Majesty's birthday was honoured by a masquerade, this year on Friday, May 20th, including the usual Magnificent Firework and Supper.'

In the same issue of *The Times* which announces this entertainment, ' Mr. Haydn respectfully acquaints the Nobility and Gentry that his Concert will be on Monday the 16th May ' in the Hanover Square Rooms, at which a New Grand Overture by Mr. Haydn will be performed. (He was to remain *Mr.* Haydn for two more months ; the Doctor's degree was conferred on him at Oxford on July 8th, 1791.)

On June 24th at Ranelagh there was ' a publick Entertainment given in favour ' of the Chevalier D'Eon. An engraving published by Boydell at the time of this entertainment describes him (her ?) as ' La Chevalière d'Eon, La Minerve

Q

Gauloise, née à Tonnerre le 5 octobre, 1728,' and at his (her ?) baptism the names were registered as Charlotte Genevieve Louisa Augusta Andrea Timothea D'Eon. In 1778 a case had been tried before Lord Mansfield involving the question of the sex of D'Eon, who had been equerry to Louis XV and had come to England as French Minister. Two foreign witnesses, one a surgeon, swore that the Chevalier was a female, and a verdict of £700 was given for the plaintiff, this being the amount of a wager laid on the subject. (After the Chevalier's death it was proved that the witnesses had perjured themselves.) D'Eon subsequently put on female attire, and when Henry Angelo called at his (her ?) house in Brewer Street he saw a ' lusty dame dressed in black silk.' Although dressed as a woman, D'Eon did not retire with the ladies after dinner, but remained to drink with the gentlemen, thus making the best of two worlds, so to speak. Among those who frequented the house in Brewer Street were J. C. Bach, Abel and Cramer. D'Eon was often at the hospitable table of the elder Angelo, in company with Wilkes and Sheridan, and helped Angelo with his treatise on fencing. They had both swordsmanship and equitation as common tastes. At the time of the Ranelagh benefit, the Chevalier was in financial straits – a not uncommon situation. In 1793 he (she) fenced in the Rotunda, as will be noted later.

On the occasion of the Chevalier D'Eon's Ranelagh benefit on June 24th, 1791, Mr. J. Ashley played solos on the organ and Master Clement on the violin. Mr. Mahon, clarinet, and Mr. C. Ashley (violinist) contributed their talents to the orchestra, and the singers were Signora Negri and Mrs. Piele (*sic*) probably Mrs. Pieltain.

Therese Negri first appeared at the fifth Salomon Concert in April. She also sang on May 30th, when Haydn's *Seven Words from the Cross* was first performed, and when it was repeated on June 10th. In the early 90's she was well known, and continued to sing at Salomon's Concerts, the Professional Concerts and the New Entertainment of Music and Dance at the Hanover Square Rooms, organised by Sir John Gallini in 1792. In the 1794–95 season she was singing at the Italian Opera, ' in the second rank.'

Mrs. Pieltain (née Chenu or Channu), wife of Pieltain, the horn player spoken of earlier, had sung at the Pantheon with Mara and Michael Kelly in 1788, and early in the year 1791 she appeared at the same house in the favourite part of Emily in *The Woodman*, but had been unable to continue in it because of ill-health.

' Master Clement ' (Franz Clement) was eleven years old at the time of this Ranelagh concert. At his benefit on June 10th, Haydn had ' conducted ' and the ' Seven Words ' were performed. Besides being a violinist of great talent, Clement had a remarkable musical memory ; he was said to have made a piano score of *The Creation* ' by ear,' and to have played long pieces from Spohr's *Last Judgement* on the piano after hearing it only once. From Haydn's *Creation* to Spohr's *Last Judgement* is a long musical journey. Half-way through this journey, so to speak, came Beethoven's Violin Concerto which was written for him, and played by him for the first time in public on December 23rd, 1806. When he returned to his native city, Vienna, he became conductor of the newly-opened Theater an der Wien, and solo player to the Emperor. He did not die until 1842.

Yet another Royal birthday was honoured at Ranelagh, that of His Majesty, and as a change from fireworks, the visual part of the entertainment consisted in MAGNIFICENT TRANSPARENCIES, executed by Mr. Edwards, Associate of the Royal Academy. In the centre was ' BRITANNIA, supporting the Medallion of HIS MAJESTY, in the left hand, and receiving LIBERTY, with her right ; at her feet, PLENTY with two GENII in Clouds, supporting the CROWN of

BRITAIN, and the PALM of VICTORY, with the motto
Rex et Amicus Patriae.' On the two sides were ' COMMERCE
and SCIENCE with their Attributes.' The preliminary puff
ends up rather tamely with ' The other Pannels are filled with
Emblems suitable to the Occasion.'

One is glad to know that this display gave general satisfaction, and was by far the grandest exhibition of the kind that
was ever seen in this country. The sceptical might have
questioned the suitability of George III being presented with
a palm of victory, but the decorative effect was doubtless good.

The day before this display Warren Hastings had given
answers to the charges made against him with a brevity and
clarity that contrasted almost painfully with the flights of
eloquence that had characterised the speeches for the prosecution. He maintained that his conduct of affairs had led to the
prosperity and security of the Indian Empire. His years of
work and danger had been rewarded with confiscation,
impeachment and disgrace. The trial was then adjourned till
the next session.

The second anniversary of the Fall of the Bastille was celebrated in some quarters, but at Birmingham there were riots,
in the course of which the mob, with cries of ' Church and
King,' destroyed the property and houses of those suspected
of sympathy with the revolutionaries. Several Dissenting
Chapels were destroyed, for Nonconformist and Unitarian
circles were naturally more radical in their political views than
' the Establishment,' or were suspected of being so. The house
and library of Dr. Priestley, with all his scientific apparatus,
was sacked. Burke still stood alone in Parliament, although
public opinion was coming round to his views. His *Appeal
from the New to the Old Whigs* issued that June did not draw a
single Foxite Whig to his side, and the Tory Pitt's attitude of
neutrality was unchanged. But thirty thousand copies of the
Reflections had been sold, and their influence on the country

at large was growing, the more so as the trend of affairs on the other side of the Channel seemed to corroborate his views.

The last Royal birthday to be celebrated in 1791 at Ranelagh was that of the Prince of Wales, for which Signori Rossi and Tessier provided an ' Order of Firing ' of the usual type. Meanwhile, concerts of instrumental and vocal music had continued to take place on Mondays, Wednesdays and Fridays.

In spite of political uncertainty, London was fuller that summer than it had been for years. There had recently been a great increase in building. Lord Camden, for instance, had just let ground at Kentish Town ' a village between London and Hampstead ' for building 1,400 houses. Indeed, London had been spreading rapidly northwards during the last fourteen years. By 1782 the village of Paddington could be said to be ' almost a part of the capital,' and houses were springing up north of ' the New Road from Paddington to Islington.' (Now Marylebone Road and Euston Road.) Yet Paddington and Marylebone were still considered healthful suburbs. Haydn went to stay in Lisson Grove, to get away from the smoke and noise of the town. Lodgings at Lisson Green were advertised as likely to suit convalescents.

*   *   *

A thick fog diminished the attendance at Ranelagh's February masquerade of 1792 (February 14th). It ' cast its baleful mist round the skirts of the metropolis about the time the carriages were moving. Many were consequently overturned, as the coachmen could not see the horses' heads, much less the road they travelled.' Only fifteen hundred masks appeared in the foggy Rotunda, where there was a red halo round the flames of the wax candles. Most of the company wore black dominos. The three Royal brothers (the Prince of Wales, the Duke of Clarence and the Duke of York) were thus attired, and

for part of the evening Mrs. Jordan ' in a crape veil ' promenaded ' between the friendly arms of the Prince of Wales and
the Duke of Clarence.' After supper ' she resigned herself
wholly to the attention of her NATURAL protector,' that is
to say, the Duke of Clarence.

Though first and foremost a comedy actress – the very
genius of comedy her age thought her – Dora Jordan deserves
affectionate remembrance in the roll of English singers. She
was untaught, ' unscientific ' as her contemporaries would
have expressed it, and was not even in the same class as Mrs.
Martyr or Miss Leary. She was a comic actress with a pretty
natural voice, and a charming way of singing such songs as
were introduced into her parts. Robson says the extent of her
knowledge of music was the power of ' accompanying herself
simply and pleasingly on the guitar.' Sometimes she sang un-
accompanied. Leigh Hunt speaks of ' her sweet, mellow and
loving voice.'

On this occasion there was performed ' An Ode in Honour
of the Marriage of Their Royal Highnesses the Duke and
Duchess of York, written by a Gentleman of a Literary Character. The Music entirely new by Signor Giordani.' Princess
Frederica, daughter of the King of Prussia, had been married
to the Duke of York in the month of November. When Haydn
went to stay at Oatlands in December, 1791, she sat at his left
hand while he played his own music, with which she had
already become so familiar in Berlin that she hummed an
obbligato accompaniment, while the Prince of Wales, at the
composer's right hand, accompanied on the violoncello. Thus
the trio continued from ten at night until two in the morning.
Haydn reported that she herself sang and played very
well.

By the time of Ranelagh's regular opening in April, 1792, the
majority of even the more liberal-minded promenaders was
convinced that the French Revolution meant the confiscation

of property, the destruction of religion, and mob-rule. Terrifying and conflicting reports came from across the Channel. It was a summer of fear, and of the muddled and emotional thinking that comes from fear.

But there were distractions. The Hastings Trial was in its last season, and the demand for tickets was as great as in its early days. *Dr.* Haydn respectfully acquainted the Nobility and Gentry with the dates of his concerts. The new Duchess of York appeared as a patroness at Ranelagh. At the opening concert, Mrs. Pieltain again sang, and there was an Italian tenor, Signor Torrigiani (or Torizziani). The band was led by Mr. G. Ashley as usual, with Mr. C. Ashley playing the 'cello.

The exhibition called Mount Aetna was first seen at Ranelagh with a scene designed by G. Marinari, on May 7th, 1792. In a special building could be seen Mount Aetna and the cavern of Vulcan, with the Cyclops forging the armour of Mars ' as described in the Aeneid of Virgil.' The Cyclops went to work to the accompaniment of music by Handel, Gluck, Haydn and Giardini, and then the smoke thickened, the crater vomited forth flames, and the lava rolled along the side of the mountain. Finally, there was ' a prodigious eruption,' finishing in ' a tremendous explosion.' A ' Forge of Vulcan ' had been a feature at Marylebone Gardens twenty years earlier, and Mount Aetna was doubtless inspired by it. It was a popular attraction at Ranelagh for many years. The building was at the bottom of the Gardens, to the left of the canal if you were facing the river.

A great event took place on Tuesday, May 22nd, the performance of Giardini's oratorio *Ruth*. Haydn was at Ranelagh that evening, and all London's musical public. The Duchess of York came with her uncle-in-law, the Duke of Gloucester. They had paid £100 each for their tickets, and yet the concert did not cover its expenses. It was the last time Giardini performed in public, and though there were moments which recalled his great days, on the whole it was a painful experience for his admirers. Haydn wrote in his diary that ' Giardini played like a pig.' (It must be remembered that when Haydn had tried to make his acquaintance, Giardini had replied he did not want to know ' the German dog.')

The singers in *Ruth* were all distinguished performers : Mrs. Crouch, Miss Parke, Mrs. Bland, Miss Poole, Master Walsh, Michael Kelly and James Bartleman. Something has already been said about Miss Poole, but the others are new to these pages.

At this stage Mrs. Crouch and Michael Kelly can scarcely be thought of apart, although their early careers ran in separate channels. Michael Kelly has left his own story, written down for him in his old age by Theodore Hook, son of the composer, James Hook. It would be rash to rely on the *Reminiscences* as an historical document. It is small wonder if he made some errors in names and dates, or ' arranged ' certain episodes in his career, as he was wont to ' arrange ' music for the stage. Mick was a good raconteur, with more sense of theatre than of history. Moreover, he himself criticised Hook's handling of the material with which he provided him. But the book makes the period live for us, more vividly than better-documented chronicles. Whether the scene be the Vienna of Mozart, the Naples of Ferdinand IV, the Paris of the Revolution and of Napoleon, or the London of the Regency, Michael Kelly always makes us feel at home. He and the many subsidiary characters he introduces become friends of ours, even if their names be wrongly spelt, and wrong dates assigned to various episodes in their careers.

He was born in Dublin in 1762, where his father was a wine merchant, and also Master of Ceremonies at Dublin Castle ' known for his elegant and graceful deportment,' and with some musical taste. The boy studied piano and singing under

Mrs. Crouch

various masters, and as ' Master Kelly ' at the age of about
fifteen appeared as Cymon in Michael Arne's *Cymon*, and
Lionel in *Lionel and Clarissa* at Smock Alley. Michael Arne
was ' at the pianoforte,' and Pinto, husband of the former Miss
Brent, led the orchestra. Silvia in *Cymon* and Clarissa in
Lionel and Clarissa were sung by Mrs. Michael Arne. Michael
Kelly also sang in Piccini's *La Buona Figluola* at Crow Street,
to replace an Italian singer who had been taken ill. He there-
upon went to Italy to study singing, at the recommendation of
Rauzzini.

The full story of his career can be read in the *Reminiscences*,
or (better still) in S. M. Ellis's *The Life of Michael Kelly*. After
studying in Naples – where Sir William and the first Lady
Hamilton took an interest in his welfare – and at Palermo,
under Aprile, he was engaged as a tenor for the Pergola at
Florence. At Leghorn on his way to Florence he met Nancy
and Stephen Storace for the first time. After a series of engagements at different theatres, he arrived in Vienna, where he and
Nancy Storace both took part in the first performance of
Figaro – Nancy as Susanna, Michael as Don Basilio and
Curzio. His description of Mozart has often been quoted :
' All the original performers had the advantage of the instruc-
tion of the composer, who transfused into their minds his
inspired meaning. I never shall forget his little animated
countenance, when lighted up with the glowing rays of genius
. . . Mozart was on the stage, with his crimson pelisse and
gold-laced cocked hat, giving the time of the music to the
orchestra.' He met not only Mozart, but Paesiello and Gluck
also. Gluck coached him in the part of Pylades, and ' superintended the rehearsals with his powdered wig and gold-headed
cane.' After the first production of *Figaro*, Kelly, the Storaces
and Attwood returned to England together, visiting Leopold
Mozart at Salzburg *en route* and seeing something of the Paris
theatres.

On April 20th, 1787, he first appeared in London as the Lionel to the Clarissa of Mrs. Crouch, and that was the beginning of their long association.

Anna Maria Phillips, better known as Mrs. Crouch, was born in London in 1763. Maria Julia Young, her pompous and often inaccurate biographer, tells us that at the age of ten or eleven she was capable of accompanying herself on the harpsichord in ' The Soldier tir'd of war's alarms.' (Even in later years she preferred the harpsichord to the new-fangled pianoforte as an accompaniment.) Her first teacher was a Mr. Wafer, organist of Berwick Street Chapel, but in her teens she was articled to Thomas Linley, father of Elizabeth Sheridan. He brought her out at Drury Lane at the age of sixteen or seventeen as Mandane in *Artaxerxes*, with the tenor Vernon as Artabanes. She seems to have acquitted herself well enough vocally, but her beauty and charm made a stronger impression than her voice. There seems always to have been a quality of touching youthfulness and innocence about her appearance and her singing, which went to the heart. She worked hard to improve her acting, which was poor. Brandes speaks of her as ' ein recht hübsches Mädchen, jedoch ohne Ausdruck, hat eine sehr gefällige angenehme Stimme im Singen, aber aüsserst wenige und schlechte Aktion.' The year that Michael Kelly and Nancy Storace began their Vienna engagement (1783), Anna Maria Phillips was singing at Smock Alley, where Michael had made his debut. In 1784 she tried to elope with the son of an Irish peer. The young people's plan was discovered ; they were overtaken, and separated by their respective parents.

On her return to London she found gossips busy with the story of her broken romance, and she suffered much pain and embarrassment. Bad poetry in praise of her charms and ill-natured tittle-tattle both appeared in the public prints. In 1785 she married Rollings Edward Crouch, a Lieutenant in the

Navy. The marriage was not a success, but there was no open breach for six years.

When she and Kelly met, they were both in their early twenties, both attractive and talented, and both eager to advance in their profession. She improved his English diction, and he gave her lessons in Italian. Their work threw them together, and soon he took up his residence in the Crouch household, an arrangement considered curious even in the eighteenth century. From 1791 the Crouch's ceased to live together. Scandal-mongers said the marriage broke up because Mrs. Crouch became the mistress of the Prince of Wales. Certainly the Prince honoured both Mrs. Crouch and Michael Kelly with his ' patronage,' and had no more loyal subject than Kelly, whose praise of the First Gentleman and gratitude for his favours are fulsomely expressed in the *Reminiscences*. The Prince had a genuine love of music, as well as of good wine and pretty women, and all three were to be found in the Crouch – Kelly home. The Crouch – Kelly partnership continued unbroken. They sang together at Drury Lane during the winter season, they travelled about in the summer fulfilling provincial engagements, they entertained guests (royal and otherwise) in Suffolk Street, Lisle Street, or (later) The Saloon, Pall Mall, and they took pupils. She died in 1805, and Kelly erected a monument to her in the old parish church of St. Nicholas, Brighton, upon which it is stated that ' She combined with the purest Taste as a singer the most elegant simplicity as an Actress : beautiful almost beyond parallel in her Person, she was equally distinguished by the Powers of her Mind. They enabled her when she quitted the Stage, to gladden Life by the Charms of her Conversation, and refine it by her Manners.' The stone was ' inscribed to her beloved Memory by him whom she esteemed the most faithful of her Friends.'

' The most faithful of her Friends ' was overwhelmed by

her loss, and soon after decided to retire from the stage, although he continued to write (or ' arrange ') music for it for many years. He also imported and sold wines in a small way, which gave rise to Richard Brinsley Sheridan's *bon mot* at his expense : ' Michael Kelly, Composer of Wines and Importer of Music.' As a singer, Michael Kelly was ' useful.' His voice had no great natural beauty, but he was a good musician, a good actor and a hard worker. He did not die until 1826, twenty-one years after his dear companion, and the same year as Charles Incledon.

*   *   *

Accounts of dead singers are often monotonous reading, and one is wearied by such phrases as ' the justness of her intonation and the elegance of her style entitled her to an honoured place in the public esteem,' or ' the rapidity of her divisions was universally admired.' But every now and then there emerges from the shadowy crowd one in whose performance there was an individual quality which is reflected in contemporary comments. Such was Mrs. Bland. Listen to Henry Phillips : ' Such pure and silvery tones surely never issued from a human throat before : this, added to the extreme simplicity of her style, threw a charm and magic around all she did that was perfectly entrancing . . . Hers was a voice never to be forgotten, and which still lingers in my ear whenever I speak of it.' Or to Robson, who said hers was ' one of those flowing voices.' The phrases almost bring her singing to life again. Almost, but alas ! not quite.

Unlike Mrs. Crouch, she had no physical attractions to help her. She was pock-marked, short-sighted, squat and thick-set. Her fine eyes seem to have been her only redeeming feature. As a child, ' Ida Romani,' daughter of Italian-Jewish strolling players, sang little Italian songs at Marylebone Gardens. She had to be perched on a table, and acquired the name of

Romanzini because of her small stature. Later she studied with
Charles Dibdin in his ' seminary to mature actors and actres-
ses ' at the Royal Circus, and appeared at that theatre in 1782.
In 1786 she first appeared at Drury Lane, as Antonio in the
English version of Grétry's *Richard Coeur de Lion* to the
Mathilde of Mrs. Jordan. In 1790 she married Bland, Mrs.
Jordan's brother. The marriage was a failure, but it was as
Mrs. Bland that she charmed the town in ' *No Song, no
supper,*' *The Iron Chest, Inkle and Yarico, The Pirates, The
Children of the Wood*, and other so-called English operas.
Jack Bannister was frequently her partner, and their joint per-
formance as Josephine and Walter in *The Children of the
Wood* was specially memorable. Besides this stage work, she
was a very popular Pleasure Gardens singer. No singer practised ' the English ballad style ' with such success as this ugly
little woman of Italian-Jewish origin. She could draw tears by
representing a street singer or beggar maid. She had a method
peculiar to herself of introducing into her comic ballads a word
or two of speaking, and then instantly recurring to the air.
Oxberry (*Annals of the Stage*) specially praises her enuncia-
tion, and says she never sacrificed sense to sound.

The accidental loss of one of her children ended her career
in 1824. She went out of her mind, and lived in obscurity until
her death in 1838.

*   *   *

Maria Hester Parke, as already mentioned, was the daughter
of one famous oboe player and niece of another. She was born
in 1775, and was one of the best-known concert and oratorio
singers of the 90's and the first decade of the following century. She is said to have made her debut as a pianist at the age
of eight, and when she was thirteen she played a concerto
' with neat and brilliant execution, together with great taste
and expression.' She played at the Salomon concerts in 1786,

and the Professional, 1791–93. There was a Miss Parke who sang among the trebles at the 1784 Handel Commemoration, which may have been Hester, but her debut as a solo singer was in 1790, when she came out at the Three Choirs Festival as ' second singer.' She sang an ' aria and scena ' at Haydn's benefit on May 2nd, 1794, among other important engagements, and continued in the front rank of singers until her marriage to John Beardmore in 1815.

*   *   *

James Bartleman, bass, was born in 1769 and died in 1821. As a boy he sang alto, or at least a low treble, in the Abbey Choir under Dr. Cooke. Letitia Hawkins says that ' Nothing more melodious ever warbled in the air.' (' Bart ' spent his leisure with the Hawkins.) He was a delicate boy, she tells us, but very amusing, with a keen sense of humour. Even in those days his voice was distinguished by its fulness, strength and ' roundness ' of tone. One of his best solos was Green's ' Acquaint thyself with God.' By the time he was eighteen or nineteen his voice had settled down sufficiently for him to sing bass in the chorus of the Antient Music Concerts, and very soon he was singing solos. He first appeared at the Three Choirs Festival at Hereford in 1792, and from then until 1817 he sang at every Festival, except when prevented by illness in 1806, 1812 and 1813. (He was never robust.)

His voice was not of outstanding beauty, but was powerful and of wide range. His out-and-out admirers praise the ' roundness ' of his tone, while the critic of the *Musical Quarterly*, 1818, considers this ' roundness ' to be obtained at the cost of distorting his vowels. But all are agreed as to the sincerity, musical qualities and imagination in his singing. The same critic in the *Musical Quarterly* says : ' . . . no man was ever more alive to his art than this gentleman. His deportment from the moment he takes his place in an orchestra

JAMES BARTLEMAN ESQ:
Gentleman of His Majesty's Chapels Royal,
Died April 15.1821 . Aged 52

O - - Lord   have mercy O Lord up - on me

Sig: Pergolesi.

displays too openly to be mistaken the genuine love he has for music. He enters with the liveliest solicitude into all the parts that are going on.' He was responsible for reviving Purcell's great bass solos, neglected since Leveridge's day, and his rendering of certain Handel airs, such as ' O ruddier than the cherry,' made a deep impression on his contemporaries. But it was his singing of Pergolesi's ' Lord have mercy upon me ' (the first notes of which are inscribed upon his memorial slab in the cloisters of Westminster Abbey) that most moved hearers. The Rev. J. W. Evans was six years old when Bartleman stayed at his parents' house, and sang ' Lord have mercy upon me,' ' standing as it were upon tiptoe, as was his wont, to give height to a somewhat diminutive stature, entrancing the ear with the pious fervour of the entreaty of the first motive of that song, and elevating the spirit by the enthusiastic burst of joyous assurance in the second, " But my hope hath been in Thee." ' The child was ' caught up weeping ' by his mother at the close of the song, and hurried off to bed. The ' impression of that night ' was never obliterated. Besides singing in concert and oratorio, James Bartleman was a noted glee-singer, and when on June 12th Ranelagh gave a grand programme of catches and glees by ' the most Favourite Performers,' we can be sure he was singing.

*   *   *

' Master Walsh ' (or Welsh) must have been about twelve at the time of the *Ruth* performance at Ranelagh. He was already singing in oratorio under Linley at the King's Theatre, while Drury Lane was being rebuilt. Mrs. Crouch, Mrs. Bland and Michael Kelly were frequently his fellow-artists. Tom Welsh had been born at Wells in about 1780, and like Charles Dibdin and Charles Incledon began his musical career as choirboy soloist. Crowds from Bath, Bristol and Bridgewater used to go to Wells on Sundays to hear him sing. Richard

R

Brinsley Sheridan heard him, and passed him on to his father-in-law, Thomas Linley. His father was a John Welsh, and there is a tradition (for which I can find no basis) that his mother was one of Thomas Linley's daughters. When his voice broke he studied music with C. F. Horn, John Cramer and Baumgarten, and from 1802 sang as a bass. He was a Gentleman of the Chapel Royal, and also composed a certain amount of music for the theatre. He became famous as a singing teacher. Among his pupils were Kitty Stephens, and Mary Ann Wilson, whom he afterwards married. He did not die until 1848, by which time the world of eighteenth-century music in which he had made his first successes – the world of Linley, Giardini and Haydn – had vanished as completely as the Rotunda.

The usual concerts continued at Ranelagh on Mondays, Wednesdays and Fridays, and for a while Italian singers appeared on Tuesdays and Saturdays in a burletta of Paesiello's (no title given). These singers included Signora Negri, already familiar to Ranelagh audiences, Signor Albertarelli and Signor Morelli, under the leadership of Mr. (*sic*) Federici. Morelli has the distinction of being the first singer to sing ' Non piu andrai ' from Figaro in this country. This was on February 4th, 1792, at the New Entertainment of Music and Dancing. (Signora Negri was also singing that evening.) He had been a footman of Lord Cowper's at Florence before his remarkable bass voice was trained. Not only had he a fine voice, but he was a good actor and had some musical taste. He was a favourite of the London public for many years.

When the King opened Parliament on January 31st, 1792, a reduction in the naval and military establishments was announced, and on February 17th, three days after Ranelagh's foggy masquerade, Mr. Pitt painted a picture of national prosperity, saying further that there ' never was a period when, from the situation of Europe, we might more reasonably anticipate a durable peace than at the present moment.' Pitt was determined to keep this country out of war, in spite of Burke and others who saw a threat to civilisation in the French Revolution. He had refused to help Austria and Prussia in their proposed crusade to restore ' sound government ' in France. When France declared war against Austria in April of 1792, he resolved on neutrality, even if Belgium should be occupied by the French armies, although he demanded that Holland should remain untouched. The French had been misled by the early enthusiasm for the Revolution among certain classes in England, and were disappointed that she was not helping them to ' emancipate ' Europe. French agents made themselves busy in the courts of the native Princes of India, they entered into correspondence with the United Irishmen, and tried to fan the dying flames of revolutionary enthusiasm in the Constitutional Clubs in this country. Events moved fast. On July 1st the French National Assembly declared that a league of Kings was formed to destroy the French Constitution, founded on the principles of eternal justice, and called upon every French citizen to defend it, with the rallying cry of ' La Patrie en danger ! ' The Duke of Brunswick's manifesto of July 25th roused French patriotism still further, and also, unfortunately, popular fury against the Royalists. There followed the massacres of August and September, which horrified every decent person in this country, strengthened the hands of Burke and his party, and doomed Pitt's non-intervention policy.

By the middle of October, the ' revolutionary mob ' had succeeded in pushing out of France the combined armies of Austria and Prussia. Not content with defending their own country, the ' nation of infernal monsters ' pushed on into the Low Countries, and promised fraternity and assistance to all who wished to throw off the yoke of tyranny. Our ally, Holland, was threatened. France could no longer be considered

VII

1793 – 1803

WAR WITH FRANCE AGAIN ; BRIEF INTERLUDE OF PEACE AND THE END OF RANELAGH

YET in April, 1793, the newspapers spoke not only of the war, but of the variety of amusements which were occupying the time and attention of the public. On Ranelagh's opening night (April 15th) another of the Mahon sisters, Mrs. Munday, made her debut in the Rotunda. The programme included orchestral music by Pleyel, Handel and Geminiani. Signor Torizziani sang again this season. The regular vocal and instrumental concerts continued, with an occasional evening of catches and glees.

At the end of June a very numerous assemblage of fashionable company, including the Prince of Wales and Mrs. Fitzherbert, saw an Assaut d'Armes between the Chevalière (*sic*) D'Eon and M. Sainville. The combats took place between the acts of the concert. The Chevalière was ' habited somewhat in the style of a Combatant of old,' and ' displayed infinite skill in the Science, which the alertness and ability of her opponent, indeed, gave her continual occasion to exhibit.' ' She ' was congratulated by the Prince.

There was no diminution in masquerades or displays of fireworks. But the Duke of York, instead of scandalising the polite world by appearing at Ranelagh in boots, was commanding the British and Hanoverian army in Belgium. And the war was not going very well. We had not yet got into our stride, but the war was still regarded as necessary, and popular feeling was violently against the Revolution. The ragged rabble of the Revolutionaries proved surprisingly good soldiers, and our forces in the Netherlands were deficient in numbers, equipment and training.

A Fire Work under the direction of M. Caillot (*sic*) was given on July 19th ' for the benefit of the Waiters.' The Order of Firing included ' A large Regulating Piece in Six Mutations,' ' Two large Dragons combatant,' several ' Flights of sky rockets,' and ' a large Bomb-shell, illuminated with Comet and Blazing Stars.'

Six days before this display, a young lady called Charlotte Corday had made her way to Paris and murdered the leader of the Jacobins, Jean Paul Marat, ' in a bathing machine.'

* * *

At Ranelagh a masquerade in April, 1794, there was at least one topical ' character ' : a ' Charlotte Cordé risen from the grave was all night brandishing her sanguinary dagger in pursuit of Robespierre, whom she vowed to Maratise in due time.' Robespierre had a few more months to run, but that other ' monster,' Danton, had fallen early in April. On the 23rd of that month Warren Hastings was acquitted, after a trial lasting seven years, two months and eleven days. Horror at the excesses in France and fear that England might go the same way made people in this country lose both their sense of proportion and their sense of justice. The natural movement towards reform, economic and political, was checked for many years to come. Moderate, far-seeing men who tried to expose social injustice and to adapt the sacred principles of 1688 to the new industrial age were accused of being atheists, revolutionaries and would-be regicides. The Habeas Corpus Act was suspended, in order that ' dangerous ' people might be dealt with more speedily. Charles James Fox and a few of his followers kept their heads. He never wavered in his belief in the saving power of justice and liberty, and opposed the measures of panic which were approved by many hitherto reasonable people. The war was going worse, and Prussia had already seceded from the Coalition.

Yet the state of Europe did not prevent Dr. Haydn from coming to England in February, and staying until August of the following year. That summer he produced his symphonies 100 and 101, known more familiarly as the Military and the Clock.

Ranelagh had its masquerades, its vocal and instrumental concerts, and its fireworks. Another share was put up for sale, and intending bidders were reminded that Ranelagh shares (being freehold) entitled their possessors to a vote for the county of Middlesex, as well as to a general ticket of admission for two persons, and a private stand for a carriage.

In the middle of the summer Robespierre fell, and France had new masters. Yet the war went on.

*   *   *

Ten days before Ranelagh opened in 1795, the shattered remnants of the British army had been evacuated from Bremen, after a disastrous retreat through Flanders. The enemy now held the entire coastline facing these shores. Our allies were dropping off, one by one, and those that still remained were lukewarm.

There was unrest in the country at large. The war was no

longer so popular, neither was the King. Taxation was heavy, and the harvest had been bad.

But London was celebrating a royal wedding, that of the Prince of Wales to Princess Caroline of Brunswick, and Ranelagh was never backward in expressions of devotion to the royal family. It was discovered that the birthday of the new Princess of Wales was on May 17th, while that of Her Majesty was on May 19th, so that a joint celebration could be staged. M. Caillot produced a magnificent 'Order of Firing.'

Clothes both for men and women had greatly changed during the past six or seven years. The doctrines of the French Revolution were partly responsible for the simplifying of costume, and for the pseudo-classical fashions. Although the English ladies did not copy the French *merveilleuses* to the extent of going about in transparent, clinging muslin chemises over pink tights, they wore high-waisted gowns that were very skimpy when compared with the voluminous hooped petticoat which (in various shapes) had been seen ever since Ranelagh's opening. The high waist seemed a particularly startling innovation. In one of James Hook's songs, a young lady pleads :–

> *Then, prithee, dear sirs, leave our short waists alone,*
> *'Tis the whim of the day, and we'll have it, don't*
> *doubt us !*
> *So give o'er your jesting, and candidly own*
> *You can't for the life of you, men, do without us !*

Shawls, muffs and fichus were used to provide extra warmth. The new modes were very chilly. Hair was no longer puffed-up or puffed-out, but arranged in loose curls, bound with a fillet or ribbon, but a fashion for wearing huge ostrich plumes on the head recalled the high hairdressing of an earlier age. Precious stones were not in keeping with the new ideas of

simplicity, and so imitation antique cameos were worn instead.
Gentlemen's clothes were simpler, too. Wigs or powdered
heads were worn only by extreme Tories who wanted to make
it quite clear they did not sympathise with the revolutionary
ideas of liberty, equality and fraternity. Sympathisers with the
Revolution, like Fox, on the other hand, affected a certain
negligence in their attire. The followers of Fox also favoured
fox-fur muffs, and wore yellow, while Pitt's Tories wore
scarlet waistcoats, and those who wished to show special
loyalty to the Throne wore ' Constitutional blue ' (as already
noted in connection with the Birthday Drawing Room of
1789). Politics and fashions were closely linked.

Ever-loyal Ranelagh celebrated the birth of Princess Charlotte on April 7th, 1796. (Three months later, her parents
were separated.) The Grand Masquerade, Supper and Firework were under the Patronage of His Royal Highness the
Prince of Wales. Private supper tables could be engaged at
Ranelagh House by the Nobility and Gentry. The supper was
by Waud and Cocks, Bond Street, and the wines – consisting
of port, champagne and burgundy – from the St. Alban's
Tavern. Tickets could be obtained from Longman Brodrip's
Music Shops, Dussek and Corri's Warehouse, Dean Street,
or Waud and Cocks. *The Times* considered that the Managers
of Ranelagh were very much ' to be commended for their
liberality in providing CHAMPAGNE for the Masquerade on
Thursday. Port, &c may be very wholesome after Dinner, but
nothing can vie with sparkling Champagne for raising the
Spirits, and provoking Mirth and Hilarity.'

The regular opening was on Friday, April 20th, when the
Fantoccini (puppets) first appeared, ' as performed under the
direction of the late Mr. Carnevale.' In their programme were :
Les Petites Affiches, *Les Deux Chasseurs et la Laitière* (*Duni*),
L'Erreur d'un Moment (*Dézède*). During Haydn's first visit to
London he went to see the Fantoccini in the Théâtre des

Varietés Amusantes, Savile Row. He recorded in his diary that the figures were well managed, and the orchestra fairly good, but the singers bad. He did not mention the names of the singers in his diary, but we do know that Mr. Mountain directed the orchestra, that Patria was first oboe, and that the programme included music by Piccini, Paesiello, Sacchini, Pleyel and Haydn himself. Haydn was something of a connoisseur in marionette productions, and wrote several operas for the Esterhazy puppet theatre between 1773 – 1778. A newspaper commented on the Ranelagh performance that ' The performers, and in particular Harlequin, went through their parts in a manner that astonished every spectator ; the action of the puppets being so very correct, and so well suited to the words. The dialogue is light and vivacious, as is usual with all French works ; the airs pretty, and the scenery and machinery of the whole admirably executed.' The Fantoccini performed regularly at Ranelagh for the next two seasons. Vocal and instrumental concerts, catches and glees and the Fantoccini provided Ranelagh's music that summer.

There had been no grand water fêtes since the 1775 regatta, but rowing competitions were still popular, and on August 12th a silver cup was given by the Proprietors ' to be rowed for by Five Pair of Oars, to start from Blackfriars Bridge at six o'clock, to row through the center arch of Battersea Bridge,[1] and back to Ranelagh Stairs.' Three Acts of Fantoccini, a Grand Fire Work, tea and coffee were thrown in by the Proprietors as good measure for the 5/- admission fee. (' Doors to be opened at seven, and the Fire Work to begin at eleven o'clock.') The entertainment was ' By Desire, and under the Patronage of H.R.H. the Princess of Wales.'

Meanwhile, young General Buonaparte was sweeping through Italy, and in October Lord Malmesbury went to

[1] Battersea Bridge had been built in 1771 to replace the Old Chelsea Ferry.

Paris to negotiate peace with the Directory. Negotiations fell
through, he was ordered to leave Paris within forty-eight hours
and arrived back in London at the end of December. Invasion
was expected in England at any time. An attempt was made by
Hoche to land in Ireland, where the United Irishmen were
ready to support him. His fleet was dispersed, but the panic
caused by it provoked the military to appalling atrocities
against the wretched Irish peasantry.

*   *   *

More cheerful news came early in 1797 when the country
learnt of Sir John Jervis's defeat of the Spaniards off Cape St.
Vincent on February 14th. Sir John was raised to the peerage,
and Commodore Nelson, who had played an important part in
the action, was knighted. But the rejoicings were only an oasis
in a desert of gloom. Invasion was still hourly expected.
(There was, indeed, an attempted landing in Wales, which was
on such a small scale, however, that it was defeated by the
country people armed with scythes and pitchforks.) French
victories in Italy and the failure of Lord Malmesbury's peace
mission caused a depression in the public funds worse than
anything felt during the blackest days of the American War.
The Bank of England suspended payment in specie, and issued
twenty shilling notes. In the navy, discontent with insufficient
and bad food, small pay, the general conditions, cruel discipline on some ships, and the inadequacy of Greenwich pen-
sioners' allowances boiled up into open mutiny at Spithead on
April 15th. There was justice in these grievances, and they
were presented with no show of violence. Nelson said he was
entirely with the Spithead seamen in their complaint. Sailors
were a neglected set, and shamefully treated when peace
came. Many nervous people saw the hidden hand of Jacobin
France in the mutiny, but there was no sympathy with French
political principles among the mutineers. They were ready to

sail to meet the French at once, if required. Indeed, their conduct was most reasonable and orderly. But the news of such a mutiny at such a time filled all hearts with dismay.

Yet on April 18th Ranelagh held a Grand Masquerade and Supper, 'with Champagne, Burgundy, Claret, Madeira, Port and Sherry.' On that day the preliminaries of peace were signed at Leoben in Styria between the Austrians and the French, and the Board was sitting in the Fountain Inn, Portsmouth, to examine into the causes of the mutiny. At the end of a week of anxiety, the country breathed again. A royal pardon was circulated through the Fleet, and satisfaction of all demands promised. The orderly Spithead mutiny was over. But less orderly mutinies were to follow, and there was still unrest in the Fleet, and a certain distrust of the Government's bona fides.

Ranelagh celebrated another royal wedding on May 25th, that of the Prince of Wurtemberg and the Princess Royal. (He had arrived at Portsmouth during the Spithead mutiny, and was cheered by the mutinous Fleet.) The Grand Gala and Bal Paré was under the immediate patronage of Their Royal Highnesses the Prince of Wales, the Duke of York and the Duke of Clarence. The Managers ventured to assure the Public that this would be one of the most distinguished Fêtes ever given in this country. The company were respectfully requested to assemble at nine o'clock. The Amusements of the evening would be varied, and would begin at ten o'clock. There were to be one hundred tables of twelve covers each, the best French and other wines, and fruits and other rarities in season. Immediately after the supper there was to be a magnificent Firework, 'with devices, emblems and decorations analogous to the occasion,' and the whole would conclude with a Dejeune (sic) in a new style. Tickets were two guineas each, and could be had at Messrs. Lockhart and Co., Bankers of Pall Mall, or at Ranelagh House. The whole was to be planned and conducted by M. Texier, whose taste was too well-known to require any eulogium. Meanwhile, the mutiny which had broken out at Sheerness was growing more and more serious, and *The Times* considered that unless some very severe measures were taken against the offenders, not merely would all discipline be at an end, but the very well-being of the State itself would be endangered. The Nore mutiny was of a different character from that of Spithead. Nelson, who had sympathised with the latter, said he would be happy to command a ship against the Nore scoundrels. The Government and the Admiralty put down the new rebellion with firmness, and by the middle of June the seamen had repudiated their ringleaders, twenty-nine of whom were executed. The abuses which had led to the Spithead mutiny, and which were undermining the whole British navy, were reformed, and in future seamen were to be treated more in accordance with their deserts.

During the negotiations, from mid-May to mid-June, the Fantoccini performed three times weekly at Ranelagh, and there were the customary concerts of vocal and instrumental music.

On June 1st there was another Grand Masquerade and Supper, and on the same day England intimated to the Directory a willingness to resume peace negotiations. Pitt said he felt it his duty as an English Minister and a Christian ' to use every effort to stop so bloody and wasting a war.' In spite of the opposition of the King, and of Burke and Windham, he convinced the Cabinet, and early in July Lord Malmesbury set out on his travels once more, to meet the French plenipotentiaries at Lille. England's position without allies was weak, well-nigh desperate, and she could not afford to drive a hard bargain for the peace she so badly needed. France controlled practically the whole of the European continent, and though she too wanted peace, she wanted it on her own terms. Negotiations dragged on during Ranelagh's summer season, until a *coup d'état* in France replaced the old plenipotentiaries with new ones whose final terms were to include not only the return of all former French, Spanish and Dutch possessions, but the surrender of the Channel Islands, Canada, Newfoundland, Gibraltar and British India. On September 18th the peace talks were abruptly broken off, and Lord Malmesbury was ordered to leave Lille within twenty-four hours. The man behind the *coup d'état* and the man who profited most by it was General Buonaparte. Soon after, he was appointed to the chief command of the 'Army of England.' The war would go on. Admiral Duncan's victory off Camperdown on October 11th was a ray of sunlight in a murky sky.

The eighteenth century, which had given England days of such splendour and prosperity, was drawing to its close in doubt and despondency. And three of its great figures passed away in that ominous year of 1797: ugly John Wilkes, who whatever his faults might have been, had fought pugnaciously and successfully for parliamentary rights and the freedom of the Press ; that other great fighter, Edmund Burke, to whom the British Constitution was sacred and the French Revolution the work of the devil, who had died protesting against Malmesbury's peace mission ; and Horace Walpole, so different from either, who shrank from all kind of violence, who was a collector of beautiful things and a shrewd, if sometimes sarcastic, observer of the social and political scene, and who to many people seems the very incarnation of eighteenth-century taste, moderation and irony. He was eighty when he died, and there can have been few living in 1797 who remembered, as he did, the opening of Ranelagh and its early days.

At the end of the year Pitt had to face a budget deficit of nineteen millions, and a further loan of fifteen millions was needed to prosecute the war. He therefore trebled (and in some cases quadrupled) the taxes on servants, horses, windows, large houses, carriages and other luxuries.

*   *   *

From a perusal of the menu for Ranelagh's Masked Ball on April 30th, 1798, one would not guess that England was fighting for her very life, against enemies without and dissension within. Supper included ' Collar'd Beef, Collar'd Veal, Ham and Tongue, Sandwiches, Pastry, Savoy Cakes, Fruit etc,' as well as ' Tea, Coffee, Lemonade, Ice Creams, Jellies, Biscuits etc.' Waud was again the ' confectioner.'

On May 18th, the day that Buonaparte set sail from Toulon for Egypt, Miss Capper and Master Elliot sang at Ranelagh. Miss Capper was a well-known singer at the end of the eighteenth century and beginning of the nineteenth, and was to sing in the first performance of Haydn's *Creation* under John Ashley (senior) at Covent Garden on March 28th, 1800. Master Elliot also sang in that performance, as did other Ranelagh artists – Mrs. Second, John Sale, Charles Dignum, and Charles Incledon. Master Elliot, who later became a well-known glee composer, studied singing with John Ashley (junior). The songs they sang on this occasion are not specified. The orchestral part of the programme consisted in works by Stamitz, Martini, Geminiani, Haydn, Bach and Corelli.

The very day after this concert, British troops made a raid on Ostend, to destroy the sluices and basins of the Bruges canal, and cut off the invasion transports which were expected by this route. They blew up the sluices, but could not re-embark owing to the wind and surf being so high, and they were obliged to capitulate to a superior force. On that same day, May 19th, Lord Edward Fitzgerald was arrested in Dublin, and on the 26th, 30,000 armed peasants rose in the county of Wexford. Massacre and arson followed. Had Buonaparte aimed at Ireland and not at Egypt, that island might have been lost, and this island also.

The trained forces in this country would have been woefully inadequate to repel invasion. Volunteers were enrolled in their tens of thousands. They had zeal and courage, but were deficient in training and weapons. There was no central command, and each corps chose its own uniform. Up and down the land they marched and drilled with martial ardour. Not far from Ranelagh, on the village green of Sloane Square the Chelsea Volunteers did their training. As in the year 1759, every able-bodied man was prepared to tackle the French ruffians if they should land. As in the year 1759, there were false reports that such a landing had taken place. But unlike the year 1759, there were no distant victories to cheer us. We had no allies on the Continent, and Ireland was a hell upon earth.

At the concert ' for the Benefit of Messrs. Ashley ' on June 1st, some of the songs had a topical appeal. Charles Incledon sang ' Sound an alarm,' and ' Come if you dare,' and the duet (with chorus) ' To arms, and Britons strike home ' with John Sale, the bass. John Sale (1758 – 1827) was a fine representative of the English Church tradition. He had been educated at Windsor (where his father was lay clerk) and Eton, and at the time of this Ranelagh concert was a lay vicar of Westminster Abbey, a vicar choral of St. Paul's and a Gentleman of the Chapel Royal. He also sang at the Antient Concerts, and was an honorary member of the Nobleman's Catch Club, of which he later became secretary. His voice was mellow and beautiful, blending well in glees, and he was a singer of taste and musicianship. Both George III and his son patronised him, and he sang at the Prince of Wales's wedding. He was also well known as a teacher. Master Elliot, Incledon, Sale, and ' Sale Junior ' sang glees. ' Sale Junior,' John Barlow Sale, was later to teach music to the Princess Victoria. Madame

Mara sang Purcell's ' Mad Bess,' and a bravura song (title not given). By request Master Elliot gave the audience Handel's ' Softly sweet in Lydian measures,' with a 'cello obbligato by Mr. C. Ashley. The instrumental music included a bassoon concerto by Mr. Holmes, who was by far the best bassoon player of his day. At that time this instrument was given far more solos than it is to-day, and was frequently used for obbligato accompaniments to the voice. Mr. Holmes was specially noted for his beautiful obbligato playing. The solo flute was a Mr. Lingo, possibly a relation of Mr. Ling, who was a well-known oboe player about the same time. Mr. W. Parke was principal oboe, Mr. Mahon principal clarinet, and Mr. Sarjant solo trumpet. Mr. G. Ashley was principal violin, Mr. C. Ashley principal 'cello, and Mr. R. Ashley (Richard Ashley, 1775 – 1836, apparently no relation of the others) principal viola. Another soloist was Dussek, the pianist. Jan Ladislav Dussek was born in Bohemia in 1760, and studied both piano and organ from his earliest years. He also gained some fame for his performances on the harmonica, but his chief reputation was as a pianist and composer for the piano-forte. He played all over Europe – Amsterdam, Hamburg, the Hague, Berlin, St. Petersburg, Milan and Paris – with brilliant success, and in 1788 the threat of coming revolution in France sent him to London. As a teacher and performer he became equally famous. In 1792 he married Sophia Corri, the singer, daughter of Domenico Corri, the singing teacher, and with his father-in-law set up a music shop and music publish-ing business. (It may be remembered that in 1796 tickets for Ranelagh's celebration of the birth of Princess Charlotte could be obtained at Corri and Dussek's Music Warehouse.) The business failed, and to escape his creditors he left England in 1800, and after a varied career died at St. Germain-en-Laye in 1812. In Hamburg he had studied with Emanuel Bach, Johann Sebastian Bach's third son, and Haydn had the warmest admiration for his talents. Early in his career Queen Marie Antoinette was his patroness, and in his last years he was in the service of Talleyrand. At the Ashley's benefit he played a ' Concerto on the Pianoforte, with a Military Rondo,' probably of his own composition. He wrote at least two military rondos, and was rather addicted to topical themes. He had written ' The naval battle and total defeat of the Dutch Fleet by Admiral Duncan, October 11th, 1797 ' and also ' A Complete delineation of the ceremony of thanksgiving for that victory,' both for pianoforte.

Tickets for this concert were only five shillings, and could be obtained from Mr. Ashley, Pimlico, the Music Shops or Ranelagh House. Patrons certainly had their money's worth on this occasion.

In June, Master Parker, aged four and a half, performed a concerto of Haydn's on the grand Pianoforte, and also recited Collins' Ode on the Passions, and the Poet Laureate's Birthday Ode.

The first volume of a collection of poems of quite another type called *Lyrical Ballads* appeared that year, written by two young men, William Wordsworth and Samuel Taylor Coleridge, but was not favourably received. The simplicity of subject and diction was revolutionary, and these poems were as different from the most admired poetry of the day as were the clothes of 1797 from those of, say, 1775. But the public will accept a change in the fashion of its dress sooner than a change in the fashion of its poetry.

For the Waiters' Benefit on July 9th, Signor Hengler directed a Grand Fire Work. The Order of Firing included ' a discharge of Sosison Vo Land (*sic*)[1] ; ' The imitative Whee of Boreas in angelic white, royal blue, green, yellow, rayonnant and brilliant fires ' ; and ' A superb Piece of Mechanism solely invented and executed by Signior Hengler, representing

[1] Query : Saussisons volants.

two Rattle Snakes in pursuit of a Butterfly (whose beautiful colours will be represented by blue, yellow, green, and other diversified fire-works); at the same time two splendid mosaics will be fixed by a flying pigeon.' Meanwhile, the main body of the Irish ' rebels ' had been defeated at Vinegar Hill on June 21st, but Ireland was still uneasy. Napoleon had landed in Egypt on July 1st, and would be in Cairo on the 22nd.

But while Signior Hengler's two Rattle Snakes were pursuing his Butterfly, Nelson and the British Fleet were pursuing the French, and on October 3rd Ranelagh was able to celebrate a victory, the Most Glorious Victory of the Nile, which had taken place on August 1st. The proceeds of the grand gala were to be devoted to the widows and orphans of the fallen. Doubtless, ladies appeared in white with ' Hail to the Victor of the Nile ! ' painted or embroidered upon their sashes and hair ribbons. London was illuminated.

*   *   *

Ranelagh tried the experiment of a January masquerade in 1799, at which the maskers drew lots for Twelfth Night Cakes. Let us hope that the fires were well banked-up in the Rotunda, for it was a severe winter. The new year opened rather more promisingly than in 1798. At the end of the old year a treaty was signed between Russia and England. Pitt had begun to build up the Second Coalition against France, which eventually included Austria, Turkey, Naples and the Two Sicilies, and Portugal. In order to pay for the proposed liberation of Europe, Pitt brought in a new financial measure – the Income Tax.

But on January 24th Naples surrendered to the French, and the Parthenopean Republic was set up in Southern Italy. Before Ranelagh's regular opening in April, the French had crossed the Rhine, and Napoleon was besieging Acre. At the grand Masquerade on April 1st, ' by Desire of several Volunteer Corps, the City Corporation Band in full uniform ' performed several ' military pieces composed expressly for the different Corps.' This type of music was understandably popular just then and was repeated at most of Ranelagh's entertainments in the summer of 1799. The King reviewed the Volunteers in Hyde Park, just as his grandfather, George II, had reviewed the ' knights of shires who had never shot at anything but woodcock ' in the year 1759. When the Inns of Court Volunteers passed, he cried : ' Call them the Devil's Own ! '

Her Majesty's birthday was honoured on May 17th with a concert and fireworks of much the usual pattern. Three days later Buonaparte was obliged to raise the siege of Acre. On June 20th, Naples was recaptured by a force of British, Russians, Italians, Portuguese and Turks under the convoy of Lord Nelson.

That August yet another raid was made on the Continent, this time on a larger scale, in the form of a combined Russian and British invasion of Holland. But after nearly two months the troops were evacuated, and the failure was the subject of mutual recriminations between the Services. To do the professional soldiers justice, they had opposed the project from the beginning, on the grounds that it was premature, but they had been overruled by the politicians, who were backed by public opinion. All through the summer there was a rising tide of martial enthusiasm and optimism in the country at large. But the Helder failure and a Russian defeat in Switzerland dashed hopes once more, and the eighteenth century went out in gloom as far as England was concerned.

But France was looking forward to a new era of glory and prosperity under the Constitution of the Year VIII, with Napoleon Buonaparte as First Consul. Weary of the futile Directory, and weary of the war, even though it had brought

them more victories than defeats, the French people wel-
comed him home from Egypt as their saviour who would
bring them peace and every other blessing. A breathing-space
in which he could gather up his forces for a decisive blow
against England was just what he wanted, and on Christmas
Day he addressed an apparently reasonable letter to King
George III, proposing peace. The only reply was a memoran-
dum from the Foreign Secretary, Lord Grenville, to Talleyrand, adverting to the origins of the war, and stating that the
French people's only hope of peace was by restoring their
ancient rulers. In other words, His Majesty's Government
would not condescend to treat with an upstart, nor did they
trust his professions. And so the war went on.

*   *   *

Ranelagh opened in January, 1800, with a Masquerade and
' A Regular Supper,' but as the inclemency of the weather
prevented a large number of ladies and gentlemen from attending, the entertainment was repeated on February 24th. Again
the Corporation Band in full uniform performed some of the
most favourite military pieces during supper.

At the Masquerade on April 17th, admission was 10/6 and
port wine 4/6 a bottle. There was criticism of the catering on
this occasion. The press considered that ' When these sort of
entertainments are conducted upon this mean and narrow
plan, the result is a vulgar and motley association.' At the
Pantheon, on the other hand, there was both quality and
quantity, and ' the wines were equal to the viands.' There
were signs, indeed, that Ranelagh's popularity was again
declining. Concerts, masquerades and fireworks continued,
however, and Miss Capper sang songs by James Hook.
Military music was popular as ever.

Gentlemen Members of the different Volunteer Corps held
a contest of marksmanship at Ranelagh on August 12th, under

the patronage of His Royal Highness the Duke of York, and in celebration of the Prince of Wales's birthday. The prize was an Elegant Silver Cup.

Meanwhile, owing to divisions in the Cabinet and a fear of repeating previous military fiascos, the chance of striking at Napoleon in his weakest spot, the Genoese Riviera, had been lost. There were no such divided councils in France and no such hesitations. Napoleon struck vigorously and decisively at Austria on the Danube and in North Italy, and on June 14th won the battle of Marengo.

The weather in England had been ideal for outdoor entertainments at Ranelagh and elsewhere, but the prolonged drought was followed by heavy rains at harvest-time. This was the second bad harvest running. In many districts there were bread riots which had to be quelled by the military. Imports of wheat were threatened by an impending stoppage of Baltic grain ships. At the end of December Russia revived against England the Armed Neutrality for the protection of maritime rights, consisting of herself, Sweden, Prussia and Denmark. Early in the same month the French victory of Hohenlinden had finally knocked Austria out of the war.

The Second Coalition was over, and at the end of 1800 Britain stood once more completely alone, with every continental port closed to her.

*   *   *

Yet January 1st, 1801, was ushered in with the ringing of bells and the firing of the Tower guns, to celebrate what some people considered the real beginning of the new century, and also the Act of Union of Great Britain and Ireland, which that day became law, having passed both parliaments and received the Royal assent in the course of the previous year. There seemed hope for Ireland at last. But the measures of Catholic emancipation which were necessary to complete the settlement were opposed by George III, who sincerely believed that by making such concessions he would be violating his Coronation Oath and betraying the Protestant Constitution he had sworn to defend. In February, Pitt resigned, after seventeen years, and with him the best men in the Cabinet. He was replaced by Addington, a mediocrity who could only find mediocrities to serve him. The agitation of the controversy brought on the King's old malady, and by the end of February he was showing alarming symptoms of insanity again.

Thus, by the time Ranelagh opened for the spring season of 1801, England was fighting for her life against the whole of Europe, governed by a king who was mad and a prime minister who was a nonentity.

Yet a newspaper account of a Ranelagh Masquerade moralises on the happy state of England compared with that of oppressed Europe : ' Happily, very happily, we are not surrounded by the factious, who, to avoid suspicion, seldom meet in public, and take advantage of a mask to carry on treasonable purposes ; this is now the case in almost every other part of Europe, and has rendered Europe herself one universal masquerade.'

The food shortage which was causing grave unrest in parts of the country was not apparent at Ranelagh. At one Masquerade not only was there an ' uncommon number of characters well supported ' – including an Othello, a Desdemona, and a female Harlequin whose figure, however, would have been more suitable to Falstaff – but ' the supper and wines were of the best quality, and in profusion.'

At another masquerade Charles Dignum, the tenor, sang. Dignum was almost exactly contemporary with Incledon, and while Incledon was making his name at Covent Garden, Dignum was singing in ' English Opera ' in the Drury Lane company. From 1784 to 1812 he was constantly before the public on the stage, in oratorio or at the Pleasure Gardens.

He, too, sang at the King's Theatre oratorios in 1792. He, too, sang in the first performance of *The Creation* under Ashley. But although he is credited with ' a fine voice,' and was evidently a useful singer, he was never on Incledon's level.

Charles Dignum was the son of a master tailor who had a business in Wild Street, Lincoln's Inn, and the boy became a chorister at the Sardinian Chapel. (The family were Catholic.) Thomas Linley made his acquaintance, and took his musical education in hand, not letting him appear in public until he considered him ready. He launched him at Drury Lane in October 14th, 1784, as Young Meadows in *Love in a Village*. In particular, he was associated with the first performance of Storace's operas – *The Haunted Tower*, 1789 : *No Song, No Supper*, 1790 ; *The Pirates*, 1792, and so on – generally in company with Mrs. Crouch, Mrs. Bland, Michael Kelly, Nancy Storace and Jack Bannister.

' Diggy ' was squat and clumsy. He and Mrs. Bland must have made a curious pair, and when Charles Lamb saw them on the stage together, he exclaimed : ' And lo, two puddings smoked upon the board ! '

' Anthony Pasquin ' will not even allow him a good voice, and ridicules his appearance as Cymon :

> *See DIGNUM trip onward as CYMON array'd*
> *Both apish and awkward, unlearn'd and ill-made.*

Like other singers of the period, he was ambitious of being a composer, and published a volume of music dedicated to the Prince of Wales, but he does not seem to have had the musical knowledge of Kelly. He died in 1827, a year after Charles Incledon and Michael Kelly.

On this occasion at Ranelagh he ' favoured the company with several charming songs during the evening which passed with glee and good humour. The saloon was elegantly lighted, the bands of music well-chosen, and " grey-eyed morn " found the company in high spirits, pleased with their enter- tainment and unwilling to depart. The supper was a very good one.' Dominoes were prevalent, but there were also several ' well supported characters.'

Catches and glees continued to be popular at the concerts that season. A name familiar to the present generation makes its appearance among the exhibitors of superb fireworks, that of Brock. Smith, Rossi, Tessier and Ruggieri are also repre- sented. In honour of His Highness the Prince of Wales's birthday, the Gentlemen of the different Volunteer Organisa- tions again shot for an Elegant Silver Cup, but out of 247 entrants, only four could find the target. The Cup was won by Mr. Tweedy ' of Blackwall and Poplar,' who paraded round the Rotunda with his fellow soldiers displaying his prize. The Rotunda was ' illuminated in a very handsome stile,' and the City Train Band Musicians played several beautiful martial airs until ten o'clock, after which the company danced country dances until eleven o'clock when the fireworks com- menced.

In connection with the last masquerade of the 1801 season (June 22nd), the SPECULUM MODORUM of 22, Fleet Street advertised that it was ' the best calculated House in London for a Masquerade Warehouse, not only for its central Situation, both for the inhabitants of the City as well as the Inns of Court ; but also from the Extension of the Premises, and the many convenient Dressing Rooms, exactly adapted for Ladies and Gentlemen . . . R. Croft, Taylor and Draper to His Royal Highness the Prince of Wales and His Majesty's Army and Navy, begs leave most respectfully to acquaint the Nobility and the Public, that he has . . . made a compleat Assortment of Ranelagh Fancy Cloak Dresses, exactly calcu- lated for Ranelagh Masquerades, being much more light and elegant than Dominos, and on as reasonable terms.' (Be it noted that Mr. Croft addresses himself to the Nobility and Public, and no longer to the Nobility and Gentry. The nineteenth century has begun.)

During the course of that summer there was seen on the silver Thames a barque which would have astonished those who took part in the 1775 Regatta, namely a steam engine which worked a barge, enabling it to make way against a strong current at the rate of $2\frac{1}{2}$ miles per hour.

Early in the spring the victories of Abercromby at Alexandria and Nelson at Copenhagen heralded the turn of the tide. Invasion seemed imminent in August, but once more the danger passed. Things no longer seemed so hopeless. But there was industrial and agricultural discontent everywhere as the result of the food situation, and everyone was war-weary. Many people felt that the Consulate was something respectable and steady, very different from the French Revolution, and that we had no real danger to apprehend from it. France had practically ceased to be Republican. And now that the offensive had passed to us, there could be no humiliation in seeking what everyone so ardently desired – peace with France.

On October 1st, 1801, Lord Hawkesbury signed the preliminary treaty with M. Otto, representing the French Government. The news was received with hysterical and uncritical joy by the country at large. But Grenville and Windham thought it the death warrant of their country. England had given up everything, everywhere. Perhaps Richard Brinsley Sheridan summed the situation up when he said it was a peace ' which every man ought to be glad of, but no man can be proud of.'

*　　　*　　　*

And so when Ranelagh opened in 1802 it could celebrate the Peace of Amiens. The Rotunda was illuminated ' with

additional Splendour,' and in the centre was erected a transparency representing the Temple of Peace, designed by Mr.
Capon. A most magnificent firework was to be exhibited, and
a hymn to peace sung, both of them replicas of those given in
Paris. It was now fashionable to admire once more the French,
who had so lately been 'the nation of infernal monsters,' and
cheers had even been heard in the streets for the First Consul,
so lately ' the Corsican Ogre.'

This was the third time in the course of its career that
Ranelagh had celebrated peace with France, and this was to be
the shortest peace of them all.

Besides the peace celebrations, Ranelagh produced in 1802
a form of entertainment so novel that the Annual Register
thought fit to comment on it in retrospect, and explain to the
uninitiated what its curious name meant. It was ' common to
the fashionable world,' and was called a Pic Nic Supper. It
consisted in a variety of dishes, each marked with a number.
' The subscribers drew lots, and each is obliged to furnish the
dish marked against his number, either bringing it with him in
his carriage, or sending it by a servant . . . The proper variety
is preserved by the taste of the Maître d'Hotel who forms the
bill of fare.' Henry Angelo ascribes a French origin to this
kind of party, at which ' the feasts were supplied by a general
subscription of viands, pastry, fruit, wine and liqueurs, each
contributing according to the dictates of their own liberality.'
But the drawing of lots was an innovation. The Pic Nic Club,
so famous at the beginning of the nineteenth century and
caricatured by Gillray, originated at a party of Lady Albina
Buckinghamshire's. Eating and drinking were not the sole
entertainment. Music and plays were performed. The patron-
esses were ladies of rank, and some of the theatricals were
purely amateur. But there were a certain number of professional actors or musicians included. Henry Angelo was an
active member of the Club, and was present at the Ranelagh

' afternoon breakfast ' on June 28th (Ranelagh was being increasingly used by Societies or clubs for giving private entertainments).

The special feature about this ' afternoon breakfast ' was a balloon ascension by M. Garnerin and Captain Sowden. (Captain Sowden was himself a member of the Pic Nic Club.)

Sowden made a statement in the course of which he said : ' As numberless questions have been put to me, respecting the sensations experienced while in the upper regions, I think it a duty incumbent on me to inform the Public, and to set them right as to the erroneous ideas they have of an aerostatic voyage . . . After we had gained the height of about 3,000 feet, I desired M. Garnerin not to ascend any higher till we had passed the metropolis, that the inhabitants might be gratified with a fair view of us.'

When they had got some small distance from the metropolis, he felt hungry and ' proposed to M. Garnerin to overhaul our lockers, where we found a ham, a cold fowl, a cake, and two bottles of orgeat. (Wines or spirits being dangerous, owing to the rareification of the air.')

They sailed happily along till they perceived Epping Forest beneath them ' like a gooseberry bush,' and realised they were heading straight for the sea. M. Garnerin said they must descend with all possible speed, so they opened the valve, but a violent squall of wind and rain hurled them with such velocity towards the earth that they feared for their lives. They were dragged along the ground for some miles, and threw out ropes to some people who came running out of a farmhouse, but these good people were ' so consternated that neither threats nor entreaties could prevail on them to come to our assistance.' A gust of wind broke the cable, M. Garnerin let go of the rope belonging to the valve, and up they went into the clouds again.

After further adventures, they landed in a field, and flung

themselves on the balloon to press the gas out of it, and prevent its rising again. Somewhat bruised and shaken, they made their way to the nearest house. M. Garnerin was wearing a ' French hat with the national cockade,' and Captain Sowden was in ' a sailor's dress,' with the Union Jack in one hand. Parliament had been dissolved that day, and the master of the house took it into his head that the two strange figures were canvassers for rival parties. ' Gentlemen,' said this free-born Briton, ' though I am a freeholder, I have made a determination not to vote for one side or the other.' Once this misunderstanding had been removed, he proved hospitable and helpful, and procured them a post-chaise to Colchester, leaving the balloon to be picked up next day. Over the site of Ranelagh some 140 years later, a balloon of a very different shape from that of M. Garnerin's could be seen floating. Could the 1802 Ranelagh crowd have been resuscitated to watch its ascents and descents, what would have surprised them most was the fact that the ropes were manipulated by figures clad in blue-grey who, although they wore trousers, were yet unmistakably of that sex which the eighteenth century invariably called fair.

Boodle's Club also gave a grand fête at Ranelagh that summer. The Rotunda was hung with the flags of our enemies ' taken in the late war,' borrowed from the Admiralty. Three bands of the Guards played during supper, which was once more provided by Waud of Bond Street, and ' did much honour to his taste and ingenuity.' A covered saloon of canvas was erected above the elm avenue in the Gardens, ' as wide as Pall Mall, and nearly twice as long as it was wide.' Lamps were hung in the trees so that ' the company walked under " an illuminated grove." ' There was a dance floor, and also a little stage for ballets, short plays, and singing. There were two transparencies ' as large as life,' one representing Britannia pointing to her commerce on the Thames, with a distant view of London, and the other ' emblematical of Peace.' By 1 a.m. there were about two thousand guests, and at one time ' the range of carriages extended to the turnpike near Buckingham House Gardens.'

The Gentlemen of the Club were in dark green coats, black capes, yellow basket buttons, white vest, and black small clothes, while the ladies were mostly in white, with green ornaments as a compliment to the Order of the Club.

In the Prince of Wales's party were the Duke of York, Prince William of Gloucester, the beautiful Duchess of Devonshire and her sister Lady Bessborough who had canvassed so ardently for Fox in the Westminster Election of 1784, Lord and Lady Melbourne, and Mrs. Fitzherbert. In the Duke of Gloucester's box was Sir Sydney Smith, who had escaped from a two years' imprisonment in the Temple, Paris, in May, 1798, and foiled Buonaparte at Acre in 1800. There were other gentlemen with them, and they ' enjoyed themselves very cheerfully till a late hour.' Among the names of ladies present – the Duchesses, the Marchionesses, the Countesses, the Dowagers and the young ladies in their first season – appears, rather surprisingly, that of Madame Récamier.

Not content with flying in the air, the people of this new century were also trying to dive into the depths of the sea, and that same year at Ranelagh Mr. Todd promised to descend into a reservoir of water twenty-five feet deep, and to remain there at the bottom for an hour. But he was ' misfitted by his coppersmith ' (his diving suit was of leather and metal), and he forgot to take down his lamp, so that he did not remain under water for more than five minutes, and the experiment was not a success.

Robert Bloomfield (1766 – 1823) recorded his impressions of a visit he made to Ranelagh during the 1802 season. Apparently he attended one of the celebrations in honour of the Peace of Amiens. The poem (published in *Wildflowers*, 1806) seems worth quoting in its entirety :–

A VISIT TO RANELAGH

To Ranelagh once in my life,
  By good-natur'd force I was driv'n ;
The nations had ceas'd their long strife,
  And PEACE beam'd her radiance from Heav'n.
What wonders were there to be found
  That a clown might enjoy or disdain ?
First we trac'd the gay ring all around,
  Ay – and then we went round it again.

A thousand feet rustled on mats,
  A carpet that once had been green ;
Men bow'd with their outlandish hats,
  With corners so fearfully keen !
Fair maids, who at home in their haste
  Had left all clothing else but a train,
Swept the floor clean, as slowly they pac'd
  And then – walk'd round and swept it again.

The music was truly enchanting !
  Right glad was I when I came near it ;
But in fashion I found I was wanting :–
  'Twas the fashion to walk and not hear it !
A fine youth, as beauty beset him,
  Look'd smilingly round on the train ;
' The king's nephew,' they cried, as they met him ;
  Then – we went round and met him again.

Huge paintings of Heroes and Peace
  Seem'd to smile at the sound of the fiddle,
Proud to fill up each tall shining space
  Round the lanthorn that stood in the middle.
And GEORGE's head too ; Heav'n screen him !
  May he finish in peace his long reign !
And what did we when we had seen him ?
  Why, went round and saw him again.

A bell rang, announcing new pleasures,
  A crowd in an instant prest hard,
Feathers nodded, perfumes shed their treasures,
  Round a door that led into the yard,
'Twas peopled all o'er in a minute,
  As a white flock would cover a plain !
We had seen every soul that was in it,
  Then we went round and saw them again.

But now came a scene worth the showing,
  The fireworks ! midst laughs and huzzas,
With explosions the sky was all glowing,
  Then down streamed a million of stars ;
With a rush the bright rockets ascended,
  Wheels spurted blue fires like rain ;
We turn'd with regrets when t'was ended,
  Then – star'd at each other again.

There thousands of gay lamps aspir'd
  To the tops of the trees and beyond ;
And what was most hugely admir'd,
  They look'd all up-side-down in a pond
The blaze scarce an eagle could bear ;
  And an owl had most surely been slain ;
We returned to the circle, and there –
  And there we went round it again.

'Tis not wisdom to love without reason,
  Or to censure without knowing why :
I had witness'd no crime, nor no treason,
  ' O life, 'tis thy picture,' said I.
'Tis just thus we saunter along,
  Months and years bring their pleasures or pain,
We sigh midst the RIGHT and the WRONG ;
  – And then WE GO ROUND THEM AGAIN !

T

Ranelagh's next and last season, 1803, brought war with France again. And before another peace came, Ranelagh was gone. No magnificent firework or superb transparency were to celebrate in the Gardens or the Rotunda the Battle of Waterloo.

Some splendid fêtes were given in the last season, although as a place of public entertainment its fashion had petered out. On June 1st took place ' a most magnificent Fête and Ball in commemoration of the Installation of the Knights of the Bath.' Once more a large temporary structure was erected in the Gardens, the entrance to it representing ' the entrance to London by Hyde Park Corner.' Once more Mr. Waud was congratulated on the supper he provided, and while the company were ' gratifying their palates with the most delicious viands,' their ears ' were penetrated with the melodious harmony of vocal and instrumental music.'

This vocal and instrumental music was provided by Charles Incledon, John Fawcett, Jack Johnstone, Denman (the actor) and Miss Howells.

' Irish Johnstone ' was one of the group of singers and actors connected with the English operas at Drury Lane, the group which included Mrs. Bland, Mrs. Crouch and Michael Kelly, Jack Bannister and Nancy Storace. When Kelly made his first appearance at Drury Lane in 1787, he found his countryman, Jack Johnstone, installed as ' first singer ' at the other Patent House. He was born about 1749 at Kilkenny, where his father was quartermaster of a dragoon regiment. One version of his career is that he enlisted at the age of eighteen in the Irish Dragoons, and when stationed at Clonmel used to climb the barrack wall at night, and serenade the daughter of a neighbouring farmer, although he was always punctually on parade the next morning. His commanding officer, Captain Brown, wanted to entertain some friends at dinner one night, and asked the Sergeant-Major who had the best voice in the

JACK JOHNSTONE

regiment. The Sergeant-Major, who knew all about Johnstone's escapades and winked at them, recommended his vocal abilities warmly. The Captain was so impressed by his singing that he gave him his discharge, and also an introduction to Ryder at Dublin. What is certain is that he made his debut as Lionel in *Lionel and Clarissa* at Smock Alley in 1773, and in 1783 made a great success of the same part at Covent Garden. His voice was ' one of the sweetest ever heard, particularly in its falsetto,' according to Robson, but it was of light weight and had not been thoroughly trained. When Charles Incledon arrived at Covent Garden, Jack Johnstone's lesser vocal powers were eclipsed, and he then developed his ' line of Irishmen.' Hazlitt speaks of his ' lubricated brogue, curling round the ear like a well-oiled moustache,' and the feeling as well as humour which he put into such character parts made them so popular with the public that there had to be an Irishman introduced into any play produced at a theatre which engaged him, or the audience would have felt itself cheated. He continued to sing ' in character,' making somewhat exaggerated use of his falsetto which was imperfectly blended with the rest of his voice. The Prince of Wales once came into his box when Johnstone was sustaining his E in alt in falsetto, and remarked ' I verily believe he has held that note ever since we were here last ! ' A fault of his was separating monosyllables into two parts. In Sheridan's *The Duenna* he would sing ' Had I a har – rat for falsehood framed,' for instance. But in his own very individual style he was a charming artist, and his portraits show him to have been a very handsome man.

In 1790 the Crouches, Michael Kelly and Jack Johnstone had gone to France together. The gentlemen kept bottles of champagne in the pockets of the travelling carriage, and drank the health of the inhabitants of every chateau they passed on the route to Paris, the two tenors ' singing all the way.' They found Paris ' all gaiety and pleasure,' and saw everything there was to be seen, including the National Assembly, where they heard Mirabeau speak. Jack Johnstone, like Michael Kelly, was very popular with the Prince of Wales, who enjoyed his Irish ballads. At the Installation Ball he favoured the company with ' Paddy's Description of Pizarro.'

Miss Howells and her sister, Miss F. Howells, were well known at Vauxhall at the end of the eighteenth century. Songs and duets by the inevitable James Hook were in their repertoire.

Fawcett, junior, whose father had sung at Ranelagh in 1755, was a character actor rather than a singer, and his name belongs rather to the annals of the stage than music. He had first appeared at Covent Garden in 1791. At Ranelagh he appeared ' in the character of a Crier ' and sang some humorous songs, including ' mock Italian songs.'

Charles Incledon sang ' a new Song to the tune of God Save the King,' which had been presented to His Majesty the day before, and ' graciously received.'

' The multitude of variegated lamps (40,000 of them) in various forms, of flowers, of branches of laurel, and every fanciful ornament, gave to the Rotunda a splendour and brilliancy it had never before possessed.' The banners of the Knights were hung over the boxes. A full band performed in the centre of the Rotunda (where the orchestra had been placed in the early days of Ranelagh), and the supper tables radiated from this central point, ' each set of tables tapering from the outside to the inside of the circle. Supper was provided for upwards of 2,000 persons, 1,800 of whom were accommodated in the Rotunda,' ' allowing a space of two feet for each person.' Nine hundred hot dishes were served, together with ' two hundred quarts of pease,' and ' every delicacy that nature and art could afford.' Grapes and cherries at eighteen shillings a pound, and strawberries at three shillings a ' thumb ' (sixteen strawberries) formed part of the dessert.

Ranelagh House *Thursday—May 5 a Ball.*

The Doors to be opened at nine

What was usually the orchestra was curtained off, and before supper was over this curtain was drawn to 'disclose' Incledon, Fawcett and Miss Howells, who sang the glee, 'The Red Cross Knights,' happily adapted to the occasion. After supper there was dancing. Elegant boxes were erected for their Majesties, jor the Prince of Wales and the Duke of York.

In order that the general public might see the beauty of the decorations, a ' Superb Masked Ball ' was given as part of Ranelagh's general attractions before the temporary structure was taken down. The admittance, including supper, wines and the whole of the refreshments, was one guinea.

Yet another infant prodigy made an appearance that summer, Miss Randles, ' The Wonderful Musical Welch Child, aged Three Years and a Half.' She is confidently described as ' the most extraordinary Genius that has yet appeared,' thus putting the prodigy who appeared in 1764 completely in the shade, not to speak of Master Parker. The eminent musicians who had admired her performance at the Concert of the Nobility were Dr. Burney, Mr. Salomon, Mr. Attwood, and Mr. Knyvett. These four gentlemen were indeed at the very top of the musical profession at that time. Of Dr. Burney no more need be said. Mr. Salomon was Haydn's Salomon. Thomas Attwood had been a friend and pupil in Vienna of the 1764 musical prodigy when that prodigy had grown up, and he lived long enough to welcome Mendelssohn to England. The Knyvett family were prominent in English music for several generations. Charles Knyvett, senior, was born in 1752, was a Gentlemen of the Chapel Royal, Secretary to the Noblemen's Glee and Catch Club, and a famous glee singer. His son, Charles, was also a singer, but was better known as an organist. He was organist at St. George's, Hanover Square, and in 1808 succeeded his father as a Gentlemen of the Chapel Royal. He edited collections of glees, and published ' Six Airs Harmonized for Three and Four Voices.' William Knyvett, born in

1779, was singing treble in the Antient Music Concerts in 1788. In 1795 he became principal alto, and two years later he too was made a Gentlemen of the Chapel Royal. He was famous as an alto glee singer in the company of James Bartleman, bass, and Samuel Harrison, tenor. In his day he was popular as a composer, and wrote the anthems for the coronations of George IV and Queen Victoria.

The very names of Mendelssohn and Queen Victoria remind us that in 1803 the world, musical and otherwise, was moving towards an age very different from that in which Ranelagh had been born and flourished. Indeed, the record of Miss Randles' performance seems to close the annals of musical Ranelagh.

On July 8th, 1803, the Rotunda was open for the last time. There was no room for it in the new world.

EPILOGUE

On September 30th, 1805, orders were given by the Proprietors for the destruction of the buildings. The furniture was sold by auction, and the organ upon which Mozart played found a home at Tetbury, Gloucester, until 1863, when it was bought by a builder, and has since disappeared. By 1807 the site was already overgrown with weeds. After various vicissitudes, the grounds were purchased by the Chelsea Hospital in 1826. In 1853 the Chelsea Bridge Road was made, to connect Lower Sloane Street with the new Chelsea Suspension Bridge (opened on March 30th, 1858), more or less following their eastern boundary, although some portion of the land was sacrificed to make the road. The new Chelsea Embankment altered the aspect of the river frontage of the Hospital and of what had once been Ranelagh Gardens.

Ranelagh House, the Rotunda, the Chinese Temple, the Garden Orchestra, the Grotto and the Temple of Pan are vanished as completely off the face of the earth as the eighteenth-century spirit which designed them, and used them as a setting for elegant fireworks, *ridottos al fresco*, Venetian masquerades and other polite entertainments. But Ranelagh's fate has been happier than that of Vauxhall. It remains a garden, although laid out on a new plan. Some of the oldest trees may have shaded the polite world of the eighteenth century, and visitors to the Chelsea Flower Show walk upon the same earth, if not the same grass, as Sterne, Reynolds, Goldsmith, Dr. Johnson, Haydn and all the others who accepted the invitation to Ranelagh.

THE END

BIBLIOGRAPHY

' *Ambulator* ' or the *Stranger's Companion in a Tour round London*, 1782.

ANDERSON Emily : *Letters of Mozart and his Family*, 1938.

ANGELO Henry : *Reminiscences*, 1828.

BEAVER Alfred : *Memorials of Old Chelsea*, 1892.

BESANT Sir Walter : *London in the Eighteenth Century*, 1902.

BOSWELL : *Life of Johnson.*

BOTSFORD J. B. : *English Society in the Eighteenth Century as influenced from Oversea.* Macmillan (New York), 1924.

BRANDES Georg : *Bemerkung über das Theater*, 1786 (Göttingen).

BRYANT Arthur : *The Years of Endurance*, 1942 ; *The Years of Victory*, 1944.

BURNEY Charles : *A General History of Music*, 1789 ; *An Account of the Musical Performances in Westminster Abbey*, 1785.

BURNEY Fanny : *Early Diary*, edited A. R. Ellis, 1907.

CARSE Adam : *The Orchestra in the Eighteenth Century*, 1940.

CARTER Elizabeth Mrs. : *Letters to Mrs. Montagu*, 1817.

COOKE W. : *Memoirs of Charles Macklin, Comedian*, 1804.

CORRI Domenico : *Select Airs, ca.* 1780.

CUMMINGS W. H. : *Dr. Arne and Rule Britannia.*

DEAN C. G. T. : *Lord Ranelagh's House in Chelsea* (Transactions of the London and Middlesex Archæological Society, New Series, Vol. VII, Part II).

DELANY : *The Autobiography and Correspondence of Mary Granville, Mrs. Delany*, 1862.

EDGECUMBE R. Lord : *Musical Reminiscences of an Old Amateur*, 4th edition, 1834.

ELLIS S. M. : *Life of Michael Kelly*, 1930.

EVANS Rev. J. W. : *Musical Recollections of the Last Half Century*, 1872.

FLOOD W. H. Grattan : *Introductory Sketch of Irish Musical History.*

FLOWER Newman : *George Frederic Handel, his Personality and his Times*, 1923.

GARDINER W. : *Music and Friends*, 1835 and 1853.

GEORGE M. Dorothy : *London Life in the Eighteenth Century*, 1925.

GRAY Thomas : *Letters*, edited Duncan C. Tovey, 1900.

GREEN J. R. : *A Short History of the English People*, 1874.

HAWKINS Letitia : *Memoirs and Anecdotes*, 1824.

HAWKINS Sir John : *A General History of the Science and Practice of Music*, 1776.

HAYES W. : *An Account of the Five Music Meetings*, 1768.

HAZLITT W. : *Works*.

KELLY Michael : *Reminiscences*, 1826.

KIDSON Frank : *Articles in the Musical Times*, 1922.

LAMB Charles : *Works*.

LANGLEY Hubert: *Dr. Arne*, 1938.

LAVER James and Iris Brooke : *English Costume of the Eighteenth Century*, 1931.

LECKY William E. H. : *A History of England in the Eighteenth Century*, 1883-1890.

LEWES Lee : *Memoirs by Himself*, 1805.

LEWIS W. S. : *Three Tours through London in the Years*, 1748, 1776, 1797, 1941 (Yale).

LOEWENBERG Alfred : *Annals of Opera*, 1597-1940, 1943.

MEE J. H. : *The Oldest Music Room in Europe*, 1911.

MELVILLE Lewis : *The Life and Letters of Laurence Sterne*, 1911.

MORITZ Carl Philipp : *Travels*, 1782, edited 1926.

NATHAN I. : *Musurgia Vocalis*, 1823.

NICOLL Allardyce : *A History of Late Eighteenth Century Drama*, 1927.

OULTON W. C. : *Theatres of London*, 1796.

OXBERRY W. : *Anecdotes of the Stage*, 1817.

PASQUIN Anthony : *The Children of Thespis*, 1792 ; *The Pin Basket to the Children of Thespis*, 1797.

PHILLIPS Henry : *Musical and Personal Recollections*, 1864.

POHL C. F. : *Mozart und Haydn in London*.

RICHARDSON A. E. : *Georgian England*, 1931.

ROBERTSON C. Grant : *England under the Hanoverians*, 1923.

ROBINSON H. Crabb : *Diary*, 1869.

ROBSON *The Old Playgoer*, 1854.

ROGERS Samuel: *Recollections of the Table Talk of Samuel Rogers*, 1856.

ROWSE A. L. : *The Spirit of English History*, 1943.

SICHEL Walter : *Sterne, A Study*, 1910.

SITWELL Sacheverell : *Conversation Pieces*, 1936.

TERRY Charles Sanford : *John Christian Bach*, 1929.

TREVELYAN G. M. : *Social and Economic History of England*, 1944.

TURBERVILLE A. S. : *English Men and Manners in the Eighteenth Century*, 1926.

TWINING : *Recreations and Studies of a Country Clergyman of the Eighteenth Century*, 1882.

WALPOLE Horace : *Correspondence*, edited Mrs. Paget Toynbee.

WALPOLE Horace : *Correspondence*, edited W. S. Lewis.

WHEATLEY H. B. : *Hogarth's London*, 1909.

WILKINSON Tate : *The Wandering Patentee*, 1795.

WROTH Warwick : *The London Pleasure Gardens of the Eighteenth Century*, 1896.

YOUNG W. J. : *Memoirs of Mrs. Crouch*, 1806.

Annual Register ; Harmonicon ; Musical Quarterly ; Georgian Era ; Contemporary Newspapers ; *Gentleman's Magazine ; Universal Magazine ; Macaroni and Theatrical Magazine ; London Magazine ; Town and Country Magazine ;* Grove's *Dictionary of Music and Musicians ; Dictionary of National Biography ;* Ranelagh Collection in the British Museum ; Own Ranelagh Collection ; Acts relating to Chelsea.

PRINCIPAL CHARACTERS
MENTIONED IN THE BOOK

MUSICIANS AND ACTORS

ARNE Dr. T. A., 1710-1778 : Composer and singing teacher. Wrote music for Ranelagh and arranged its concerts (especially in the 1760's).

ARNE Cecilia, *née* Young, 1711-1789 : Singer, wife of Dr. Arne.

ARNE Michael, 1740-1786 : Composer, son of Dr. Arne. Also wrote music for Ranelagh.

ARNE Mrs. Michael (1), *née* Elizabeth Wright, died sometime before 1773 : Singer. Sang at Ranelagh, 1763, 1767, 1768.

ARNE Mrs. Michael (2), died early nineteenth century : Singer.

ASHLEY J., died 1805 : Musician, chiefly bassoon. Ranelagh, 1789, etc.

ASHLEY G. C., *ca.* 1770-1818 : Violinist. Son of J. Ashley. Ranelagh, 1789, etc.

ASHLEY C. J., 1773-1843 : Cellist. Son of J. Ashley. Ranelagh, 1791, etc.

ASHLEY J. J., 1772-1815 : Organist, pianist and singing master. Son of J. Ashley. Ranelagh, 1791, etc.

ASHLEY R., 1775-1836 : Viola player. Ranelagh, 1798, etc. (All the Ashley's were connected with Ranelagh music at some time from 1789 onwards.)

AVISON Charles, 1710-1770 : Composer. Concerto performed at Ranelagh, 1789.

BACH J. C., 1735-1782 : Composer. Son of Johann Sebastian Bach. Music often performed at Ranelagh.

BADDELEY Mrs. *née* Sophia Snow, 1745-1801 : Actress and singer. Sang at Ranelagh, 1769, etc.

BAILDON Joseph : Composer. Wrote songs for Ranelagh, 1760, etc.

BANNISTER Charles, 17 ? -1804 : Bass. Sang at Ranelagh, 1770.

BARTHELEMON Mrs., *née* Polly Young, *ca.* 1749-1799 : Singer. Niece of Mrs. T. A. Arne. Sang at Ranelagh, 1789, etc.

BARTHELEMON François Hippolyte, 1741-1808 : Composer and violinist. Husband of Mrs. Barthelemon, friend of Haydn.

BARTLEMAN James, 1769-1821 : Bass. Sang at Ranelagh, 1792, etc.

BEARD John, 1716(?)-1791 : Tenor. Sang at Ranelagh, 1749, and for many years.

BLAND Mrs., *née* Ida Romanzini, 1769-1838 : Singer. Sang at Ranelagh, 1792.

BOYCE Dr. William, 1710-1779 : Composer. Wrote music for Ranelagh.

BRENT Charlotte, later Mrs. Pinto, died 1802 : Singer, pupil of Dr. Arne. Sang at Ranelagh in the 60's, etc.

BROWN Abram : Violinist. Succeeded Michael Festing at Ranelagh *ca.* 1752.

BURNEY Dr. Charles, 1726-1814 : Organist, composer, writer on music, played organ at Ranelagh, 1771.

CHAMPNESS : Bass. (First singer of Heart of Oak, 1759.) Sang at Ranelagh, 1762, etc.

CLEMENT Franz, 1780-1842 : Violinist (born in Vienna). Played at Ranelagh, 1791, as ' Master Clement.' In 1806 gave the first performance of Beethoven's violin concerto (written for him) in Vienna.

CROUCH Mrs., *née* Anna Maria Phillips, 1763-1805 : Singer and actress. Sang at Ranelagh, 1792.

DIBDIN Charles, 1745-1814 : Composer, singer, actor. Sang at Ranelagh, 1767, etc., and wrote music for Ranelagh.

DIGNUM Charles, 1765(?)-1827: Tenor. Sang at Ranelagh, 1798, etc.

DUSSEK J. L., 1760-1812 : Pianist, composer (born in Bohemia). Played at Ranelagh, 1798.

FESTING Michael, died 1752 : Violinist. Led the band at Ranelagh, 1742-*ca.* 1752.

FORMANTEL (Fourmantel) Kitty : Sterne's ' Dear Jenny.' Ranelagh, 1760.

FRASI Giulia : Handelian singer. Sang at Ranelagh, 1751, **1752**.

GARRICK David, 1717-1779 : Actor. At Ranelagh, 1772, etc. Wrote words for Ranelagh song, 1768, music by M. Arne.

GIARDINI Felice de, 1716-1796 : Violinist. His ' Ruth ' performed at Ranelagh, 1792.

HAYDN F. J., 1732-1809 : Composer. Visited Ranelagh, 1792.

HOOK James, 1746-1827 : Composer. Wrote much for Ranelagh.

INCLEDON Charles, 1763-1826 : Tenor. Sang at Ranelagh, 1789, etc.

JOHNSTONE Jack ('Irish Johnstone '), 1749-1828 : Singing actor. Performed at Ranelagh, 1803.

JORDAN Mrs. Dora, *ca.* 1762-1816 : Singing actress, mistress of the Duke of Clarence, later William IV. Visited Ranelagh, 1792.

KELLY Michael, 1762-1826 : Tenor. Sang at Ranelagh, 1792.

LINLEY Thomas the Elder, 1732-1795 : Singing teacher, composer, manager of Drury Lane Theatre. Father of Elizabeth Linley (Mrs. Sheridan).

MAHON W. and J. : Leading clarinet players (brothers) during the last 20 years of the eighteenth century.

MAHON The Misses, later Mrs. Munday, Mrs. Ambrose, Mrs. Warton and Mrs. Second : Singers, sisters of the above. Mrs. Second first appeared at Ranelagh (as ' Miss Mahon ') in 1786, etc., and Mrs. Munday in 1793.

MARA Mme., *née* Gertrude Elizabeth Schmähling, 1749-1833 : Singer. Sang at Ranelagh, 1790, etc.

OSWALD James, *ca.* 1710-1769 : Scots composer. Wrote for Ranelagh from 1761.

PARKE John, 1745-1829: Oboe player. Played at Ranelagh, 1789, etc.

PARKE W. T., 1762-1847: Oboe player, composer and author of *Musical Memoirs*. Brother of the above.

PARKE Maria Hester, 1775-1822: Singer. Daughter of John Parke. Sang at Ranelagh, 1792.

PARRY John: Blind Welsh harper, bard to Sir W. W. Wynne during mid-eighteenth century. Played at Ranelagh, 1746. Died Ruabon, 1782.

PASQUALINO Cellist. Played at Ranelagh, 1764.

PIELTAIN Dieudonné-Pascal, 1754-1833: Violinist. Played at Ranelagh, 1789, etc.

PIELTAIN Mrs., *née* Chenu: Singer. Sister-in-law of D. P. Pascal. Sang at Ranelagh, 1791, 1792.

POOLE Maria, later Mrs. Dickons, *ca.* 1775-1833: Singer. Sang at Ranelagh, 1789, 1790.

REINHOLD 1737-1815: Bass. Sang at Ranelagh, 1775.

SCOTT The Hon. Mrs. John, *née* Isabella Young, *ca.* 1739-1791: Singer. Niece of Dr. Arne's wife. Sang at Ranelagh in the 60's.

STANLEY John, 1713-1786: Blind organist and composer. Played at Ranelagh, 1755.

TENDUCCI Ferdinando, *ca.* 1736-died early nineteenth century: Soprano singer and composer. Sang at Ranelagh in the early 60's, and also wrote songs for Ranelagh.

VERNON Joseph, 1738-1782: Tenor and composer. Sang at Ranelagh, 1775.

YOUNG The Misses: See Arne, Barthelemon, Scott.

AUTHORS

BURNEY Fanny, 1752-1840: Daughter of Dr. Charles Burney (see Musicians) Novelist (later Madame D'Arblay). Visited Ranelagh, 1771, etc.

BOSWELL Alexander, 1740-1795: Advocate, essayist, traveller, wrote the *Life of Samuel Johnson* (published 1791) which speaks of Ranelagh.

CARTER Mrs. Elizabeth, 1717-1806: 'Bluestocking.' At Ranelagh, 1742.

GIBBON Edward, 1737-1794: Historian and politician. Entered parliament 1774, where he supported Lord North. *The Decline and Fall of the Roman Empire*, vol. I, published 1776, vols. II and III, 1781, and the last three volumes, 1783.

GOLDSMITH Dr. Oliver, 1730-1774: Novelist, poet, playwright. At Ranelagh, 1772, etc.

GRAY Thomas, 1716-1771: Poet. At Ranelagh, 1746, etc.

FIELDING Henry, 1707-1754: Novelist, essayist, playwright, political journalist, Justice of the Peace for Westminster. Speaks of Ranelagh in *Amelia* (1751). In his *Enquiry into the Late Increase of Robbers* he denounces both gin and masquerades.

JOHNSON Dr. Samuel, 1709-1784: Essayist, lexicographer. Visited Ranelagh, 1772, etc. (See Boswell's *Life*).

RICHARDSON Samuel, 1689-1761: Novelist.

ROGERS Samuel, 1763-1855: Banker, verse-writer. Ranelagh mentioned in his *Table Talk*.

SHERIDAN Richard Brinsley, 1751-1816: Dramatist, also politician. (See Politicians and Statesmen.)

SMOLLETT Tobias, 1721-1771: Novelist, essayist, historian. Speaks of Ranelagh in *Humphry Clinker* (1771).

STERNE Laurence, 1713-1768 : Parson and novelist. At Ranelagh, 1761, etc.

WALPOLE Horace (later Lord Orford), 1717-1797 : Collector, writer on art, letter-writer. Frequently at Ranelagh. Son of Sir

Robert Walpole, Whig Prime Minister (see Politicians and Statesmen). College friend of Thomas Gray.

WHITEHEAD William, 1715 - 1785 : Poet and dramatist. Poet Laureate 1757.

ARTISTS AND ARCHITECTS

CANALETTO (Antonio da Canale 1697-1768) : In England 1746-1748, when he painted Ranelagh, and other London scenes.

CHAMBERS Sir William, 1726-1796: Architect. (Somerset House, the Pagoda at Kew.)

CHIPPENDALE Thomas, died, 1779 : Furniture-maker. Author of the *Gentleman's and Cabinet-maker's Directory*, published 1754.

GAINSBOROUGH Thomas, 1727 - 1788 : Painter. Painted portraits of many of Ranelagh's patrons.

HOGARTH William, 1697-1764 : Painter, engraver of social and political satire.

JONES William, died, 1757 : Furniture designer, architect to the East India Company, architect of the Rotunda at Ranelagh.

REYNOLDS Sir Joshua, 1723-1792 : Painter. Not only painted portraits of many of Ranelagh's patrons (*e.g.*, the Ladies Waldegrave, exhibited at the Royal Academy, 1787) but was also himself a visitor to Ranelagh.

THE ROYAL FAMILY

GEORGE II, 1683-1760. Frequented Ranelagh in its early days.

GEORGE III, 1738-1820. Son of Frederick, Prince of Wales.

QUEEN CHARLOTTE, wife of George III, 1744-1818. Celebrated the recovery of George III at Ranelagh, 1789. Her birthday frequently celebrated at Ranelagh.

' THE PRINCE OF WALES ' (1) Frederick, Prince of Wales, 1707-1751. Son of George II, and father of George III. Quarrelled with his father.

' THE PRINCE OF WALES ' (2) 1762-1830. Eldest son of George III. Later, the Prince Regent, and finally, George IV. Married Mrs. Fitzherbert privately 1785. Married Caroline of Brunswick, 1795.

' THE PRINCESS OF WALES ' (1) Augusta of Saxe Gotha, died, 1772. Wife of Frederick, Prince of Wales, and mother of George III.

' THE PRINCESS OF WALES ' (2) Caroline of Brunswick, 1768-1821. Married The Prince of Wales, 1795. Princess Charlotte born, 1796. Separation, 1796.

PRINCESS CHARLOTTE, 1796-1817. Only daughter of Prince and Princess of Wales. Her birth celebrated at Ranelagh.

THE DUKE OF CLARENCE, third son of George III (later William IV), 1765-1837. At Ranelagh, 1792.

THE DUKE OF GLOUCESTER, son of Frederick Prince of Wales, and brother of George III, 1743-1805. Married Maria, Countess of Waldegrave, niece of Horace Walpole and mother of the Ladies Waldegrave. At Ranelagh in 1769, 1780, 1792, etc.

THE DUKE OF YORK, 1763-1827, second son of George III. Commander - in - Chief, 1795-1809, 1811-1827. At Ranelagh, 1789.

THE DUKE OF CUMBERLAND (1) 1721-1765. Son of George II, victor of Culloden.

THE DUKE OF CUMBERLAND (2) 1745-1790. Son of Frederick Prince of Wales and brother of George III. At Ranelagh, 1769, etc.

THE DUKE OF CUMBERLAND (3) fifth son of George III, 1771-1851. Later King of Hanover.

CHRISTIAN VII, of Denmark, 1749-1808. Married Caroline Mathilda, daughter of Frederick, Prince of Wales and sister of George III.

Divorced her, 1772. In England, and at Ranelagh, 1768.

PRINCE FREDERICK OF WURTEMBERG. Married the Princess Royal, 1797. Ranelagh celebrated their wedding, and they both patronised its entertainments.

PRINCE CHARLES EDWARD STUART ('Bonnie Prince Charlie,' 'The Young Pretender,' 'The Boy'), 1720-1788. Landed in the Hebrides, July, 1745. Defeated by the Duke of Cumberland (q.v.) at Culloden, April, 1746.

SOLDIERS AND SAILORS

BYNG Admiral John, 1704-1757. Failed in his attack on the French fleet off Minorca; tried, condemned and executed, 1757.

CLIVE See Politicians and Statesmen.

HAWKE Lord Admiral, 1715-1781. Defeated the French at Quiberon Bay, 1759. First Lord of the Admiralty, 1766-1771.

JERVIS, John, Earl St. Vincent, 1734-1823. Defeated the Spanish fleet off Cape St. Vincent, 1797. Suppressed mutiny in the Channel, 1797.

NELSON Horatio, Viscount, Admiral, 1758-1805. Battle of the Nile, 1798. Copenhagen, 1801. Trafalgar, 1805.

RODNEY Lord Admiral, 1718-1792. Destroyed the Spanish fleet, 1780. Defeated the French fleet, 1782.

SMITH Admiral Sir Sidney, 1764-1840. Escaped from two years' imprisonment in the Temple, Paris, 1798. Foiled Bonaparte at Acre, 1800. At Ranelagh (Boodle's Fête) 1802.

WOLFE James, General, 1726-1759. Dettingen, 1743. Quebec, 1759.

THE DUKE OF CUMBERLAND See The Royal Family.

THE DUKE OF YORK See The Royal Family.

STATESMEN AND POLITICIANS

ADDINGTON Henry, 1757-1844: Premier, 1801-1804, on the resignation of Pitt. The Peace of Amiens was signed during his reign, and its failure caused his fall and the return of Pitt.

BURKE Edmund, 1729 (1730?)-1797: Politician, orator. Opposed

American taxation, 1774. Brought in charges against Warren Hastings (q.v.) 1786. Broke with Fox and his fellow-Whigs on the issue of the French Revolution, which he (Burke) vehemently opposed. Published *Reflections on the Revolution in France*, 1790.

BUTE Lord, 1713-1792 : Prime Minister, 1762-1763. His influence with the Dowager Princess of Wales made him very unpopular. Under him, Parliament was becoming a mere tool of the young King, George III. Attacked in the *North Briton* by Wilkes, 1762. On his resignation he was succeeded by Lord Grenville (*q.v.*).

CLIVE Robert, baron of Plassey, 1725-1774 : Defeated Surajah-Dowlah at Plassey, 1757. Governor at Calcutta, 1757. Governor of Bengal, 1765. Commission of enquiry into his conduct and administration, 1773, and debate in the Commons, which voted he ' had rendered great and praiseworthy services to his country.'

FOX Charles James, 1749-1806 : Politician, orator. Joined the Whigs, 1774, and opposed the American policy of Lord North and George III. Aided in the prosecution of Warren Hastings (*q.v.*), 1786. Supported the principles of the French Revolution, and opposed the war with France, hence his break with Burke (*q.v.*).

GRAFTON Duke of, 1736-1811 : Secretary of State in the Rockingham Administration 1765-1766. Premier 1767-1770. Succeeded by Lord North (*q.v.*).

GRATTAN Henry, 1746-1820 : Irish orator and statesman. Opposed English rule, and demanded the power of taxation for Ireland, 1780. Advocated Catholic Emancipation, 1791. Opposed the Rebellion, 1798. Opposed the Union, 1799.

GRENVILLE Lord, 1712-1770 : Succeeded Lord Bute, 1763. Introduced the American Stamp Act, March, 1765. Resigned, July, 1765. Succeeded by the short-lived Rockingham Ministry (*q.v.*).

HASTINGS Warren, 1732-1818 : Virtual Governor of British India, 1772. Governor General, 1774-1785. Trial ' for high crimes and misdemeanours,' 1788-1795. Acquitted, 1795.

HAWKESBURY Lord, 1770-1828 : Foreign Secretary under Addington, 1801-1804. Signed the preliminaries of the Peace of Amiens, 1801.

MALMESBURY Lord, 1746-1820 : Ambassador to France, Spain, etc. In October, 1796, and September, 1797, he went on fruitless peace missions to France.

NEWCASTLE Duke of, died, 1768 : Succeeded his brother, Henry Pelham (*q.v.*) 1754-November, 1756, when the disasters of the Seven Years War drove him from office to be replaced by Pitt. On Pitt's resignation, April, 1757, he attempted unsuccessfully to form a government, and 1757-1762 joined with Pitt (*q.v.*).

NORTH Lord, 1732-1792 : Premier, 1770-1782, and with George III, largely responsible for the events leading up to the American War. The disasters in America and the state of affairs in Ireland caused his fall in 1782, which was a personal defeat for the King himself.

PITT William the Elder (afterwards Lord Chatham), 1708-1778: As one of the ' Young Patriots ' opposed Sir Robert Walpole's peace policy. Secretary of State, November, 1756-1757, in succession to the Duke of Newcastle. Resigned, April, 1757 (driven from office by the enmity of George III and Newcastle), but in July, 1757, joined Newcastle in forming a government, in which he was to be responsible for the conduct and successful issue of the war. Earl of Chatham, 1766. Opposed the American policy of the King and Lord North, 1774-1777.

PITT William, the Younger, 1759-1806 : Son of the above. Chancellor of the Exchequer, 1782. First Minister, 1783, until his resignation, 1801. 1804, until his death, again First Minister. He was against interference on the Continent, and opposed war with France until public opinion and force of circumstances made it inevitable.

PELHAM Henry, 1695-1754 : Led the opposition against Sir Robert Walpole, and caused his fall, 1742. First Minister, 1743, until his death, when succeeded by his brother the Duke of Newcastle (*q.v.*).

ROCKINGHAM Lord, 1730-1782 : Succeeded Lord Grenville, 1765 (July) until May, 1766, when he was succeeded by Pitt (Lord Chatham). First Minister, March 1782, in succession to Lord North, when he was responsible for bringing to an end the disastrous American war and for pacifying Ireland. He died July, 1782, before the humiliating peace was signed.

SHELBURNE Lord (later Marquis of Lansdowne), 1737-1805 : Foreign Secretary, March-July, 1782. First Lord of the Treasury (on the death of Lord Rockingham, *q.v.*), July, 1782- April, 1783.

SHERIDAN Richard Brinsley, 1751-1816 (see also under authors) : Spoke at the trial of Warren Hastings, 1787. Held various Government posts. Friend of the Prince of Wales (later George IV), and a supporter of Fox.

WALPOLE Sir Robert (afterwards Lord Orford), 1676-1745 : First Lord of Treasury and Chancellor of the Exchequer, 1715-1717 and 1721-1742, *i.e.*, Prime Minister, although the term was not used until 1742. He was largely responsible for the consolidation of the Hanoverian dynasty, and the development of the Cabinet system of government, and his policy of peace at all costs kept this country out of European entanglements for twenty years. But in 1739 he was obliged to consent to war with France and Spain over our trading interests (The War of Jenkins' Ear), and in February, 1742 he was defeated in the Commons, became Lord Orford and ceased to be a Minister of the Crown. His peace policy had been increasingly opposed by the ' Young Patriots ' (see William Pitt the Elder), and by the trading interests, and with the death of Queen Caroline in 1737 he had lost powerful support. He was succeeded by Henry Pelham (*q.v.*).

WILKES John, 1727-1797 : M.P. for Aylesbury, 1757. Founded the *North Briton*, 1762, which attacked Lord Bute (*q.v.*), and in ' No. 45,' King George III himself. He was expelled from the House of Commons, 1764 ; elected for Middlesex, 1768, with ensuing riots ; again expelled, and twice re-elected. Lord Mayor, 1774.

WINDHAM William, 1750-1810 : Secretary at war under Pitt, 1794-1801.

OTHER NOBILITY AND GENTRY

BESSBOROUGH Lady (earlier Lady Duncannon) *née* Henrietta Spencer, sister of the Duchess of Devonshire, died 1821 : Canvassed for Fox in the Westminster Election. In the Prince of Wales's party at Boodle's Grand Fete at Ranelagh, 2nd June, 1802.

CHESTERFIELD Lord, 1694-1773: Author of 'Letters to his Son.' At Ranelagh, 1744, etc.

CHUDLEIGH Elizabeth, 1720-1788, later Countess of Bristol, and bigamous Duchess of Kingston: Said to have been the original of Thackeray's Beatrice Esmond. Appeared as Iphigenia at the 1749 Masquerade. Tried for bigamy, 1776.

DEVONSHIRE Duchess of, *née* Georgiana Spencer, 1757-1806: Friend of Fox and the Whigs. Canvassed for Fox in the Westminster Election, 1784, together with her sister Lady Duncannon. Often at Ranelagh, *e.g.*, at Boodle's Grand Fete, 2nd June, 1802, in the Prince of Wales's party.

FITZHERBERT Mrs., 1756-1837: Privately married to the Prince of Wales (later George IV) 1785. At Ranelagh, 2nd June, 1802 (Boodle's Grand Fete), etc.

GORDON Lord George, 1750-1793: Caused the No Popery riots, 1780. Tried for high treason and acquitted, 1781. Professed Judaism, 1786.

GUNNING Elizabeth, *ca.* 1734-1790: 1752 married James, Sixth Duke of Hamilton, who died, 1758. 1759 married John Campbell, Marquis of Lorne, heir to the dukedom of Argyll. 1770 became Duchess of Argyll. She and her sister, Maria, were the sensation of London in 1751 when they first came from Ireland. 'The Double Duchess' was remarkably beautiful even in old age. At Ranelagh, 1752.

GUNNING Maria, *ca.* 1733-1760: Married George William, sixth Earl of Coventry, 1752. Died of consumption, 1760.

MELBOURNE Lord, 1744-1828: Lord of the Bedchamber to the Prince of Wales. At the Boodle's Fete, 1802.

MELBOURNE Lady, died, 1818: Wife of the above. Their son, Peniston Lamb, married Lady Caroline Ponsonby (Byron's Lady Caroline Lamb) in 1805, and as Viscount Melbourne was Prime Minister to Queen Victoria.

ROBINSON Sir Thomas, M.P., 1700-1777: Chief shareholder of Ranelagh, and Director of its entertainments. Amateur architect. Governor of the Barbadoes, 1742-1747.

TOWNSHEND Lady, died 1788: Said to have been the original of Fielding's Lady Bellaston in *Tom Jones*. At Ranelagh, 1744, etc.

WALDEGRAVE The Ladies: Greatnieces of Horace Walpole, daughters of the Dowager Lady Waldegrave, later H.R.H. Duchess of Gloucester (*q.v.*). Admired at Ranelagh, 1780. Their portrait by Reynolds exhibited at the Royal Academy, 1787.

DIVINES AND PREACHERS

DODD Dr., 1729-1777: Executed for forgery against Philip Stanhope, to whom he was tutor.

WESLEY John, 1703-1791: Founder of Methodism.

WESLEY Charles, 1708-1788: brother of John Wesley. Also Methodist preacher, and hymn writer.

WHITEFIELD George, 1714-1770: Methodist preacher.